Praise for *Reflections...*

"The contributors to *Reflections...Classroom* provide readers with a host of practical insights into and hows of developing blended learning environments. Their stories and experiences are a 'must read' for faculty and instructional designers alike. Michael Starenko and his colleagues have provided a great service to all who support pedagogically sound uses of technology in teaching and learning."

—Anthony G. Picciano, City University of New York Graduate Center

"What an amazing resource! To document, collect and share the lessons learned from blended learning pioneers is powerful from the historical perspective, and an invaluable wealth of information and source of best practices from the practitioner's perspective. *Reflections on Blended Learning: Rethinking the Classroom* is primer of case studies for blended learning faculty, instructional designers and those of us interested in effective faculty development."

—Alexandra Pickett, SUNY Learning Network

"This is the first book that provides on-the-ground examples of effective blended learning practices for instructors. The case reports document the transformation of face-to-face classrooms into cooperative environments that respond to the needs of contemporary students and the strategic initiatives of colleges and universities. This is a much-needed addition to the literature on blended learning.

—Charles D. Dziuban, University of Central Florida

"This is a much needed and timely book addressing one of the crucial transitions occurring in higher education today. *Reflections on Blended Learning* highlights and details how recent technologies and pedagogies, in the hands of motivated faculty, are transforming teaching and learning. Anyone who has considered developing a blended course or program will benefit from reading this excellent and highly useful account from successful practitioners."

—Peter Shea, SUNY Albany

Reflections on Blended Learning:
Rethinking the Classroom

Reflections on Blended Learning: Rethinking the Classroom

Perspectives and strategies from RIT faculty on how to leverage online technology to increase interaction and engagement

Michael Starenko, editor

Rochester, NY

Published by Lulu.com

© Copyright 2008, Rochester Institute of Technology, Online Learning

(cc) BY-NC-ND

This work is licensed under the Creative Commons Attribution Non-Commercial No Derivatives (by-nc-nd) License. This work may be shared, copied, distributed and transmitted, for non-commercial purposes only. This work may not be altered, transformed or built upon. To view a copy of this license, visit http://creativecommons.org/licenses/by-nc-nd/3.0/ or write to Creative Commons, 171 2nd Street, Suite 300, San Francisco, CA 94105.

Editor:
Michael Starenko, RIT

Editor, production manager, cover and layout designer:
S. Joanna Bartlett-Gustina, Earthscribe. www.earthscribe.com

Photographers:
A. Sue Weisler, John Rettallack, Educational Technology Center, RIT

Cover photography:
Markus Gann, Darko Draskovic and Johanna Goodyear, Stockxpert.com, HAAP Media Ltd.

Printed in the United States of America

First Printing: October 2008

Library of Congress Control Number: 2008935540

ISBN 978-0-557-00497-3

Contents

Introduction	1
Acknowledgements	7
Business	9
Business Information Systems Processes	10
Business to Business eCommerce	15
College Math for Business	19
Database Management Systems	23
Global Issues	28
Human Resource Information Systems	30
Internet Marketing	36
Management of Financial Institutions	41
Microeconomics	45
Principles of Marketing	49
Professional Sales Management	53
Project Management	57
Sales Management	61
Self Promotion and Business	64

Communications   69
Effective Technical Communication   70
History of Communication Technologies   73
Interpersonal Communication   76
Science Writing   79
Speechwriting   83

Computing and Information Sciences   85
Access and Accessibility   86
Advanced Routing   88
Formal Methods of Specification and Design   91
Interactive Narrative/Writing for Multimedia & New Media Perspectives   95
Managing Cyber Threats to Critical Infrastructure Protection   99
Quantitative Methods of Delivering Usable Software   102
Software Engineering I   106
Web Design and Implementation   109

Deaf Education   111
Electrical/Mechanical Design CAD   115
Introduction to the Field of Interpreting & Discourse Analysis for
Interpreters   112
Programming II in Visual Basic   121
Teaching Deaf Learners with Secondary Disorders   117
Written Communication II   124

Humanities   129
Academic English   130
Arts of Expression   134
Ethics in the Information Age   140
History of Women in Science and Engineering   143
Immigrant Voices in American Literature   146
Writing and Literature I   149

Imaging Arts and Sciences — 153
Design History Seminar — 154
Graduate Forum — 159
New Media Publishing — 164
Tone and Color Analysis — 166
Western Art and Architecture — 168

Science and Engineering — 173
Anatomy and Physiology I — 174
Biochemistry Conformation and Dynamics — 178
Math Thought and Processes — 182
Plastics Processing Technology — 185

Social Sciences — 187
Cultural Diversity in Education — 188
Energy Policy: Special Topics — 191
Fear of Crime & Corrections — 196
Foundations of Sociology — 201
History and Systems of Psychology — 204
Introduction to Psychology — 210
School Psychology Practicum — 214

Glossary — 223

Author Index — 226

Introduction

by Michael Starenko

The development of telecommunication technologies and pedagogies in the 1980s—principally those associated with the asynchronous discussion board—not only allowed distance education to be transformed into online education, but also created new opportunities for students to interact and be engaged with peers, faculty and content both inside and outside of the classroom. The important benefits of outside-of-class online interaction became increasingly apparent and appreciated around 2002-2003, and for these reasons:

1. Learner-centered or active models of instruction were moving to center stage

2. The contentious debate over "classroom vs. distance education" was subsiding

3. A critical mass of universities had become accustomed to using a courseware management system, such as Desire2Learn or Moodle, which bundle a variety of web-based communication technologies into one package

4. Students were recognized as knowledgeable about and comfortable with online technologies

5. The need for greater flexibility in scheduling our work and studies was widely acknowledged

6. An international educational movement emerged and adopted the name "blended learning" (or "hybrid learning")

The aim of blended learning is, quite simply, to join the best of classroom face-to-face learning experiences with the best of outside-of-class online learning experiences. As Randy Garrison and Norman Vaughan wrote in *Blended Learning in Higher Education* (Jossey-Bass, 2008), the "basic principle [of blended learning] is that face-to-face oral communication and the online written communication are optimally integrated such that the strengths of each are blended into a unique learning experience congruent with the context and intended educational purpose." In collaborative group work, for instance, it may be advantageous for groups to initially meet face-to-face to establish trust. In contrast, discussing a complex problem or case study that requires reflection and negotiation may be better accomplished through an online discussion board.

As blended learning has grown, so has the scholarly literature. In addition to Garrison and Vaughan's recent study, other important books on blended learning include *A Classroom of One*, by Gene Maeroff (Palgrave, 2003); *The Handbook of Blended Learning*, edited by Curtis Bonk and Charles Graham (Pfeiffer, 2006); and *Blended Leaning: Research Perspective* (Sloan Consortium, 2007), edited by Anthony Picciano and Charles Dziuban. In addition to these and many other books, hundreds of articles have been published in various print and online venues. With only a few exceptions—notably by several faculty members from the University of Wisconsin at Milwaukee writing for the journal *Teaching with Technology Today*—the scholarship on blended learning has been written mostly by educational researchers using traditional quantitative or "mixed" (quantitative and qualitative) methodologies and by instructional experts offering "how to" advice.

This book, *Reflections on Blended Learning: Rethinking the Classroom*, is likely the first to address blended learning entirely from the faculty-practitioner perspective. In particular, it brings an established form of pedagogical scholarship—personal accounts of change—to bear on this new and potentially transformational pedagogy. Maryellen Weimer, in her pioneering study of pedagogical scholarship, *Enhancing Scholarly Work on Teaching and Learning* (Jossey-Bass, 2006), invented the term "personal accounts of change" to describe a distinct category of scholarship in which faculty report experiences associated with instructional change. "These reports often begin with how the faculty member came to make this particular change," writes Weimer. "More central in this work is the change itself—it's described in detail, along with the logistics involved in its implementation."

The 54 reports collected in this book fall easily within Weimer's personal-accounts-of-change genre—to one degree or another, all describe how blended learning changed their authors' approach to teaching and learning. These reports recount how their authors discovered or encountered blended learning, the reasons they decided to adopt the blended format, how they redesigned and taught their blended courses, and how students responded to this new mode of learning. Most were written days or weeks after their authors had offered their first blended course, and therefore reflect the immediacy of recent experience.

Although *Reflections on Blended Learning* includes reports by faculty from seven of the eight colleges at Rochester Institute of Technology (RIT), we have not organized the book by college, but rather by broad disciplinary categories ranging from information technology to deaf education to the humanities. Within and across these categories are other important differences, most often at the course level (for instance, does the pre-blended course meet in the evening once a week for four hours, or twice a week during the day). This organization deliberately calls attention to the incredibly complex and inventive process of adaptation, which as Weimer notes, "is knowing how to adapt a technique...so that it fits the content, context, and instructor..."

These reports have their origin in two blended-learning initiatives sponsored by RIT's Online Learning department between fall 2003 and spring 2008. The department launched a Blended Learning Pilot Project in fall 2003. Building on its success, Online Learning rolled out a Blended Learning Program in 2005. While the two initiatives differ in name (one cannot run a "pilot" indefinitely), they were both based on the same principles and practices. As this book went to press in October 2008, 124 full-time and adjunct instructors and 187 new and unique blended courses (for a total of 323 blended course sections) participated in the two initiatives.

Both the pilot and project were based largely on the expectation that asynchronous, Internet-based communication technologies and pedagogical strategies—the same technologies and strategies that were developed in RIT's successful distance/online leaning programs—could be adapted for traditional classroom courses. We wanted to show on-campus faculty how they could use online technologies and strategies to increase interaction and engagement outside and between classroom meetings.

Within the context of both projects, a blended course was defined as any course in which approximately 25 percent to 50 percent of lectures and other face-to-face classroom activities is replaced by instructor-guided online learning activities—primarily text-based online discussion (large and/or small group)—but also synchronous web conferencing, as well as online quizzes, games, discovery labs and simulations. While so-called "seat-time reduction" was the normal expectation, it was not absolutely required for participation in the pilot or program. Participants were expected, but again not required, to use myCourses, RIT's campus-wide course management system.

Faculty received exactly the same incentives to join the pilot and the program: (1) new faculty received a one-time $500 stipend; and (2) both new and returning faculty received comprehensive course design and myCourses support from the staff of Online Learning.

The same three methods were used to recruit faculty in the pilot and the program. These methods included:

1. Faculty Workshop on Blended Learning. The first introductory workshop was held during RIT's Faculty Institute on Teaching and Learning (FITL) in May 2003. Various versions of this workshop (initially half-day, and subsequently two-hour versions with lunch) were offered once a quarter during both the pilot and the program. The early workshops were longer and more academic than later workshops, which were increasing informed by "best practices" invented by pilot and program faculty

2. Invitation to myCourses "heavy hitters." A myCourses heavy hitter is a course with a relatively large number of online discussion posts, news items, and other messages (as averaged per course participant)

3. Invitations to RIT faculty who were teaching or have taught online courses

4. In the second year of the pilot and throughout the program, invitations were sent to all faculty teaching once-a-week evening courses

Once accepted into the pilot or program, participating faculty were expected to:

1. Complete and submit an online "Blended Application" form

2. Work with an Online Learning instructional designer to develop their blended course

3. Learn the myCourses course management system

4. Inform their department chair that they will be offering a blended course

5. Attend a "Blended Luncheon" in the quarter in which they are teaching their blended course

6. Allow Online Learning to survey their students at the end of the course

7. Write a 750-1000 word report on their experience with blended learning

Participants were not formally asked to write reports until fall 2004, the start of the second year of the pilot, though several first-year pilot participants did write reports for a panel presentation at the spring 2004 FITL. Although no writing style was mandated and no template was provided (though sample reports were informally circulated among the participants), most participants used the familiar academic triad of objectives-methods-results to organize their reports.

Of the 124 RIT faculty members who participated in the pilot and program, 72 submitted reports to Online Learning. Throughout the summer of 2008 we attempted to reach all authors to obtain written permission to publish their reports; we also gave authors the option of writing a postscript to their original report. Some of these authors have left RIT or otherwise could not be reached; several authors declined the invitation. In the end, 54 authors formally granted us permission to publish their writing in this book.

Michael Starenko is an instructional designer in the Online Learning department at the Rochester Institute of Technology. He directed the department's Blended Learning Pilot and Program projects, and coordinates its ongoing blended learning initiatives. Michael has presented and written widely on blended learning, and is the lead author of "Enhancing Student Interaction and Sustaining Faculty Instructional Innovations through Blended Learning," a chapter in *Blended Learning: Research Perspectives* (Sloan Consortium, 2007). His background is in media studies, a field in which he has authored more than 100 articles and served as editor-in-chief of *Afterimage: The Journal of Media Arts*.

Acknowledgements

In preparation for this book I have been helped by many colleagues, and it is a great pleasure to express publicly to all of them my warmest thanks.

First and foremost, I am indebted to Joanna Bartlett-Gustina at Earthscribe, my superb editor, who coordinated the entire permissions, production, copy editing and layout process from beginning to end. What's more, she devised the book's title and subject matter organization, and designed its smart front and back covers.

I want to thank everyone at Online Learning who assisted me with the Blended Learning Pilot Project (2003-2005) and Blended Learning Program (2005-2008), especially director Joeann Humbert, whose enthusiastic support for these projects has made an enormous difference; and Richard Fasse and Karen Vignare, who helped to plan and research the projects, and co-facilitated many of our workshops on blended learning.

This book, of course, would not have been possible without the many Rochester Institute of Technology faculty members who contributed reports, or "blended narratives" as we informally called them, as part of their participation in the two blended projects. Thank you for sharing your experiences with blended learning with the readers of this book.

As always, I am grateful to my wife, Dale Davis, for her unwavering support, affection and love.

Business

Koffi N'Da
Business Information Systems Processes
Decision Sciences and Management Information Systems Department
College of Business
2005-2006 winter quarter

Background
Business Information Systems Processes focuses on providing students a comprehensive overview of management information systems, their tactical, operational and strategic importance, and how they affect and relate to business processes of the organization. In this course, students are exposed to many different types of information systems, related state-of-the-art technologies and management practices.

Objectives
In the past, the course was taught as a four-hour, once-a-week, face-to-face evening course. Given the variety and somewhat complexity of topics covered in this course, students found this traditional way of teaching exhausting.

The main objectives of adopting the blended approach were:

- Reduce classroom time by giving the opportunity to students to realize some of the course requirements outside the classroom, mainly online

- Make the course a learning community where students can investigate their own course topics, and share their findings with their classmates

Method
Each course session was divided into both online and in-class activities. Online activities were performed prior to class meetings through myCourses and the Clipboard survey tool. In-class activities were performed in the classroom during weekly face-to-face meetings.

Online activities
The online portion of the course focused on various activities. For me, the instructor, these activities included:

- Posting class materials to myCourses including PowerPoint presentations, materials about the group project, the individual assignment, weekly assignments, class examples, etc.

- Posting feedback on students' homework

- Uploading students' grades in the gradebook

- Creating online discussion forums for teams

- Interacting with students through e-mail and online discussions forums

- Creating online surveys for class sessions evaluation

> *"Having immediate feedback to homework and online discussions increased students' awareness of mistakes they made. This resulted in improved quality of homework, online discussions, and group project papers."*

I also extensively used myCourses electronic mail (e-mail) capabilities to communicate with students.

Online learning activities performed by students included:

- Viewing and reading course materials

- Getting fully involved in group project teams' online meetings and discussions

- Submitting homework through myCourses

- Posting questions to myCourses about confusing/misunderstood course materials

- Answering other students' questions

- Completing class evaluation surveys

In order to enhance students' participation to both in-class and online activities, I created discussion teams and a corresponding online discussion board for each team. Each team was composed of four students. A team leader was assigned each week to each discussion team according to the alphabetical order of the last name. Each discussion team member was required to be involved in classroom and online activities in order to get full participation grade.

More specifically, each discussion teammate was required to: (1) individually respond to reading questions I assigned weekly; (2) post their responses to the team's discussion board on myCourses by noon each Sunday; and (3) work collaboratively online (through the discussion board) with the team leader and other teammates to reach a consensus summary of team members' opinions about the reading questions. The discussion team leader then was required to post the consensus summary to the discussion forum on myCourses by Monday at midnight. A one-point grade was attached to each student contribution. Additionally, the team leader was rewarded with two points.

Teams of three students each were assigned a group project. Each team was required to choose and produce a research paper on a specific topic from a list I provided on myCourses and make an in-class presentation on this topic. I created a private online discussion board for each project team. Teammates were asked to use their discussion forum when fulfilling the group project's requirements. Activities that were required to be performed through the teams' discussion boards included: scheduling meetings, discussions about the group project, exchanging files, etc.

In addition, I required students to use myCourses online chat for group project interaction. I created chat rooms for group project teams. Each student contribution to group project activities was assessed based on results of a peer-review process (performed on myCourses) and the student's effective use the group project team's discussion board and/or online chat room in fulfilling project's requirements.

In addition to discussion teams and group project teams' discussion boards, I created a dropbox for each course assignment. Students were required to upload their assignments and projects (except the exams) into the appropriate dropbox. Assignments submitted outside myCourses were not accepted. I provided feedback about each submitted assignment through the dropbox. I also created a discussion board for each class session where students could ask questions about topics covered in this session. Finally, I posted individual student's grades for all assignments to the gradebook.

After each class session, I created an online survey using Clipboard to allow me to assess students' understanding of course materials covered during the session, and to take immediate corrective actions as needed. Each student was required to take the online survey.

Online participation was worth nine percent of the final grade. Each student's online participation was evaluated based on:

- The student posting his responses to weekly readings questions on time

- The student working online with the team leader and other teammates to provide a consensus summary of team members' opinions about the reading questions

- The discussion team leader posting the consensus summary on time

- The energy of the student, to ask appropriate questions online and respond to questions, comments and issues which each fellow students and the instructor raised online

"The blended learning approach reflected what many business professionals are experiencing in today's business world – both in online and physical interactions."

In-class activities

At the beginning of each weekly face-to-face meeting, I spent 15 to 30 minutes re-explaining concepts students didn't understand from the previous class session as reflected in their responses to the Clipboard survey. Then, I required each discussion team to share (with the whole class) their thoughts about the reading questions they discussed online. Each team was allowed to comment on other teams' ideas. My role in this process was to moderate students' interactions. At the end of the reading questions discussion, I shared my own responses with the class and answered questions from students. I established the link between the reading questions and the materials to cover, and performed the following activities: Lectures, demonstrating IT/IS and showing how these technologies can be used to support business processes.

In order to help students better understand the materials and their applicability, I assigned them a case study dealing with the various topics covered. Students were required to work on the case study in class with their discussion teammates, and present their solution to the entire class. Again, I played a moderator role during the discussion of the case study.

Classroom participation was worth eight percent of the total grade. Each student's classroom participation was assessed according to three criteria:

1. The student getting ready for each class by performing all assigned readings

2. The student's attendance at each and every class session on a timely basis

3. The energy of the student, to ask appropriate questions in class, and respond to questions, comments and issues that fellow students and the instructor raised in class

Results

Teaching this course in a blended format provided many advantages. First, I was able to reduce each class session from four hours to three hours by the end of the quarter due to the fact that students were accomplishing many of the course activities online.

Second, the blended learning approach reflected what many business professionals are experiencing in today's business world—both in online and physical interactions. This balance of online and face-to-face interaction allowed the class to spend more time in reflective and collaborative discussions.

Third, immediate online feedback to students' homework and to online discussions increased students' awareness of mistakes they made. Students were able to take corrective actions quickly. This resulted in improved quality of homework, online discussions, as well as group project papers.

Fourth, overall, I can say that the blended approach adopted in my class improved students' appreciation of the course as reflected by their evaluation of the course, which was better than the previous quarter.

Modifications

I expect to continue using the blended approach in this course and expand it to other courses I'll teach in the future, as this approach seems to be an effective one. Additionally, I intend to introduce other sophisticated online tools, such as the Breeze/Connect web conferencing system, in my class in order to improve the quality of online interaction.

A lesson I learned during the quarter was that having two teams (one for online discussion and another for the group project) was confusing for students at least at the beginning of the quarter. I intend in the future to create one group to perform both activities.

Koffi N'Da is an assistant professor in the decision sciences and management information systems department in the E. Philip Saunders College of Business.

James Brenyo
Business to Business eCommerce
Management, Marketing and International Business Department
College of Business
2005-2006 spring quarter

Objectives

As an adjunct faculty with a full-time job that required out of town travel and after-hours business meetings, I found it difficult to accommodate certain class schedules. All of the sessions I teach are evening classes lasting four hours. The idea of offering a blended course consisting of on-campus and online sessions was first suggested to me in the spring of 2002 by my department chair as a way of dealing with the scheduling problem that I anticipated in the summer quarter of that year. The weeks where I could not be on campus were designated as online sessions; the other weeks would be a traditional class.

Since that summer quarter of 2002 I have taught this course either in a full online format or as a blended course consisting of five on-campus meetings and five online classes. Until recently, this format has afforded me the schedule flexibility that I needed to incorporate teaching at RIT with my full-time job at Xerox.

Method

There are four areas that the online tools in myCourses were used for:

- Communicating course content for weeks when the class did not meet on campus

- Establishing an online asynchronous dialogue about the content of the lesson for that particular week

- Establishing an online asynchronous dialogue about the content of the required reading assignments for that particular week

- Establishing an area where students working on their group project could share information and progress with other members of their group in a secure environment

Students were provided with a course outline and syllabus at the beginning of the quarter that laid out how all of the content would be covered, what the requirements were and which weeks would be on-campus and which weeks would be online.

The course work consisted of 10 lecture modules of PowerPoint slides. Each module dealt with a specific topic pertaining to Business to Business eCommerce and all of the slides had speaker notes. In addition to the lecture material, two research papers and a group project were also required and there were reading assignments associated with each module. These reading assignments consisted of articles that pertained to the content of the particular module that was being taught.

The on-campus sessions consisted of a review of the PowerPoint slides (lecture) for that week with in-class discussion about the topic. If the prior week was an online session, the class began with a brief re-cap of the topics covered online and key points from the reading articles. This got students back up to speed and ready to build on what they had already learned.

For online sessions, the PowerPoint slides and required reading articles were posted in myCourses by Monday of that week. An asynchronous discussion was established for students to post questions about the slides and another discussion was established for students to post comments about the reading articles. As the instructor, I tried to check each discussion forum a minimum of once a day to review and comment (if appropriate) on what the students had posted. I also tried to prompt additional online discussion by asking provocative questions, either in the discussion forums or via e-mail.

I established a separate discussion forum for each group project team to use for collaboration purposes for their project. Students were encouraged to use this area to share concepts, draft presentations, etc., with other members of their group. Access to each group discussion board was limited to members of that particular group—other students were not permitted to see what the other groups are doing.

Results

Informal student surveys and discussions have shown that most of the students were receptive to this format. Many said that they were apprehensive at first but that the format grew on them the more they used it. In particular, they liked the convenience of doing the online work as their schedule permitted while also having the security of knowing that within a week or two at most we would meet in person and any lingering questions could be addressed at that time.

In the spring 2006 quarter, the class makeup was mostly full-time MBA students. They had a bit of difficultly getting started with the online portion of the class, even though many of them had used myCourses previously. I established the discussion forums for questions on the slides and comments on the reading, but no one posted anything. After the first week of non-participation, we discussed this in our next on-campus meeting. The students said they were afraid of posting something because "they didn't know what I wanted." Their request was that when I established a particular discussion forum that I put out a question for them to address that was related to the content associated with that discussion, e.g. "The article says that ABC will be phased out in favor of XYZ, yet that hasn't happened yet. Why not?" Once I did that, online participation began to improve. I also made a deliberate effort to reply to students' posts with additional comments and questions so as to promote more online dialogue. This method improved the results, although they were still below what I have experienced with other classes.

"There are some students that warm to the technique immediately and are uninhibited in their style, and there are students that prefer to sit on the sidelines and watch."

Postscript

I did not teach a course of any type at RIT after the spring 2006 quarter until the spring 2008 quarter. I again opted to use blended learning because working and communicating online is a vital part of how B2B e-Marketing (the subject of the course I was teaching) is done. Plus, it fit in better with my full-time work and travel schedule. I alternated between on-campus sessions and online sessions every other week.

I posted PowerPoint slides with speaker notes and associated reading assignments in myCourses during the online weeks. Students were instructed to download the slides, review them using the speaker notes and do the reading assignments. Then they were to go back into myCourses and post their comments and questions on discussion forums that I had established for this purpose. They could do all of this at a time that was convenient for them as long as it was done before we physically met for the next class.

My experience with this group was consistent with what I observed previously. There are some students that warm to the technique immediately and are uninhibited in their style, and there are students that prefer to sit on the sidelines and watch. These students required reminders and urging to get involved. It was interesting to see that in one particular case a student that was quite vocal and participatory in the classroom seldom engaged in any online discussions even after being prompted to do so.

Every class that I have used blended learning with has been unique, but in general students fall into the "bell curve" syndrome: on the one extreme there are prolific writers that need to post a comment about everything and on the other extreme there are students that seldom write anything. Both extremes tend to warrant intervention by the instructor. The majority, is in the middle of the curve, seem to do just fine. Overall the class said that they got as much out of the online weeks as they did from the on-campus weeks.

James Brenyo is an adjunct professor in the management, marketing and international business department in the E. Philip Saunders College of Business.

Birgit Coffey
College Math for Business
Center for Multidisciplinary Studies
College of Applied Science and Technology
2006-2007 fall quarter

Background
I have more than eight years of experience teaching mathematics classes in the classroom at RIT and other institutions. The class times varied from 50 minutes four times per week to the marathon four hours in one evening. I also have taught online courses where my students never had a chance to meet me in person. For each type of class, I have had students who thrive and those who do not.

From my experience, all students do not learn math alike. Some students need a problem modeled for them. They need to complete examples in an environment that provides immediate feedback for each step. The learning is modeled for them and they attempt to replicate what they have seen. This type of student lies at one end of the continuum and is often very satisfied with the structure of a classroom experience.

Some students can digest the material from the textbook fairly easily. They learn from independently completing many examples and homework problems. They enjoy tackling a challenging problem and can use examples to model a process. This type of student lies at the other end of the continuum and is often bored by the structured classroom experience.

Most students lie somewhere in between these two types of students. These students find some topics challenging and others fairly easy. They decide where to focus their energy based on how challenging the topic is. They sit and watch when the material is merely a review and dig their heels in when the material challenges them.

After many years of teaching adult students once a week, I have learned that four-hour classes are a challenge to teach in and a challenge to learn in. Since many topics in math are cumulative, a four-hour class is often divided in the following way:

- Time is spent at the beginning answering questions and/or homework from the previous week
- Foundation material is presented and examples are done
- Material builds on foundation material and more examples are done

- Application problems are introduced
- Students take a break to eat and recharge
- Application problems are tackled
- Closure is brought by addressing the connection between all the material
- Questions are answered

The material gets progressively more challenging and the learning gets more complex at the same time that the students' energy is being depleted and their ability to focus decreases.

In a traditional four-hour evening class, I would lecture and engage the students for three hours. The remaining time would be used for questions at the beginning, break in the middle, and the questions at the end. Some students would seek help during office hours, but many would not be able to see me since they work during the day.

Method

I chose to redesign the four-hour College Math for Business class in the hopes of improving both teaching and learning. Students were provided all the notes that would be presented in class. The notes were handwritten by me and were introduced with a typewritten narrative. Supporting material such as PowerPoint presentations and interactive websites were also provided.

Students were asked to work through the notes and examples each week (beginning on Sunday). A weekly quiz was due on the following Saturday.

Once students tackled the foundational material and examples, they were invited to study sessions on Tuesday and Thursday evenings to tackle material that they found challenging. If a student could complete and understand all examples and homework, then they were not required to come to the study sessions.

Half of my students came to the study sessions religiously and the other half earned grade-A work without needing my assistance. Of the half that came to all study sessions, only one-half had spent time working through the foundation material ahead of the study session. They were regularly reminded that the study sessions were most effective if they already had determined which material challenged them.

The blended course provided a study session from 5-6 p.m. on Tuesday evenings and from 5-7 p.m. on Thursday evenings. The class was originally scheduled on Thursdays from 6-10 p.m.

One student worked and could only come from the 6-7 p.m. hour on Thursdays. Other students were more flexible.

"From my experience, all students do not learn math alike. I have also learned that four-hour classes are a challenge to teach in and a challenge to learn in."

When students had tackled the foundation material ahead of time, the study sessions were able to be targeted to the more challenging material. I quickly realized that I needed a way to monitor that they had tackled the foundation material prior to meeting. Unfortunately, I was not able to access the appropriate software at that stage of the quarter. The class was small enough (under 10 students) to give each student one-on-one attention during the study session. I designed group activities to promote discussion and collaboration, but many students had differing needs. In the end, students experienced both one-to-one and group learning during the study session.

Modifications

Since this experience, I have switched textbooks so that I now have software that can help students complete the foundation material and provide me a system of monitoring whether they have done it. If I am to offer another blended class, I would use this textbook and supporting software. I look forward to teaching a blended class again soon.

Postscript

Since offering the blended math class, I have adopted a textbook and online homework delivery system—Math XL. One year after my original Blended Pilot class, I found myself back in the classroom and back in the same situation—teaching a four-hour class from 6-10 p.m. one night per week. I remembered my experience from the year prior and made some different choices.

First, during my first blended course, I contacted each student ahead of time to be sure they wanted to be part of a blended course, knowing that the in-class time would be shortened. I did not do this the second time around. Instead, I taught the first night of the class as I always do—clear, concise lessons, opportunities to ask questions, small group work, multiple activities, etc.—and only after the class was done, did I speak to them about the blended "option."

I had decided that the range of math abilities and learning styles that I encountered in this particular math course would not allow me to blend the course as I had previously. Instead, I told students that if they completed and earned an A on the homework associated with the lessons before the lessons were taught, they did not have to come for the lesson. I explained the challenges of learning mathematics in a four-hour block class and explained how Math XL provided another option. Students indicated that they felt the four-hour fatigue and that the option to learn the material before class was appealing.

During the first few weeks of the course, 10 percent of the class regularly completed the homework with an A grade and came to class only to take the quizzes. One student chose to stay for the lesson and told me that it was extremely helpful to complete the work ahead of class and hear the lesson. She had a deeper understanding of the material after putting in the time on her own and also listening to my explanation and participating in my activities. Once midterm time arrived, all students were attending all of the lessons. The material in my class was becoming more and more challenging. In addition, this was happening in the other courses students were taking and time to devote to each subject was limited.

Students appreciated the opportunity to learn the material on their own, show mastery by completing the online homework, and have the option of attending the lesson. Since then, I have used this model in the MBA Math Review courses I teach, as well as in two additional math courses I work with. This model works well because it is optional. Students all come in with a unique math background and learning style. The addition of an online homework delivery system with step-by-step examples, videos and animations provides the out-of-classroom support that many math students need.

Birgit Coffey is a mathematics instructor in the Academic Support Center in the Division of Student Affairs and an adjunct professor in the Center for Multidisciplinary Studies in the College of Applied Science and Technology.

Pam Neely
Database Management Systems
Decision Sciences and Management Information Systems Department
College of Business
2005-2006 spring quarter

Background
I used a blended format for my Database Management Systems class during the spring quarter of the 2005-2006 academic year. The focus of this course is on the design and implementation of relational database systems, along with a thorough understanding of SQL, the language of databases. The course content is roughly split in half, with the first half of the course dedicated to design concepts and the second half focused on SQL.

The course meets twice a week in a lab setting. Each student has their own work station. I had taught this class each quarter for the last three years and felt like it was a strong course. I had been considering a blended course format for some time and felt like this was a good quarter to try it. There were two motivating factors. The first was that I had been experimenting with the Breeze/Connect web conferencing system in my face-to-face classes for the previous two quarters and I felt that this was a good tool for facilitating online learning. Secondly, I knew I would be out of town for at least two class sessions and teaching the class in a blended format would allow me to incorporate my travel plans without disrupting the flow of the class.

Objective
From conversations with colleagues who were teaching online and blended courses I knew that it was important that students feel a connection with the faculty member and that they were not "teaching themselves." A major focus in adapting this course to the blended format was trying to achieve that balance of facilitating student learning and encouraging them to use the out-of-classroom time to engage in meaningful activities.

This is a course that cannot be learned by osmosis. Students must spend a significant amount of time practicing design concepts and writing SQL queries in order to learn the material. I have traditionally given students a significant amount of lab time to learn SQL and have been faced with the "we are teaching ourselves" backlash from students. My hope was that using the blended format would make it self-evident that until they do the work they cannot learn the material.

Method

Although the students understood from the first that this was a blended course, the actual organization of the course was not decided until after the course started. I was out of town for the first class meeting so I put the slides on myCourses and sent out an e-mail alerting the students to the fact that the first face-to-face class would not be held until the second session. Unfortunately, two or three students did not get the e-mail and/or didn't look at myCourses, so there was some confusion.

Approximately 60 percent of the classes were taught face-to-face. The rest of the classes were taught with a combination of synchronous Breeze/Connect sessions and additional assigned homework exercises.

There was one student in the class who was "double booked", i.e. he was taking my DBMS class from 10 a.m. to noon on Tuesdays and Thursdays, and another course from 9 a.m. to noon on Thursdays. As much as possible, I tried to accommodate his schedule, scheduling out-of-class sessions on Thursdays as often as possible. All three exams were scheduled for a Thursday and he took the exams from noon to 2 p.m. after his other class.

The synchronous Breeze web conferencing sessions typically involved a case study and development of a diagram. I used the chat feature to keep everything text based—this has the advantage of slowing me down and also avoids the complication of having to close-caption dialog. I used the white board to diagram and also used the screen sharing feature to demo Access procedures and SQL commands. I only used PowerPoint slides once—the interactive nature of the session was more useful than lecturing.

I set up groups in myCourses for each project team. This was more or less successful. The main advantage of the discussion groups was the ability to upload Access files—they cannot be easily e-mailed through the RIT system so it made file sharing much easier.

I started out asking weekly discussion questions but they were not very good questions and the discussions were limited to what you might find on a short answer test. The biggest discussion was actually initiated by a student and dealt with the date of the final exam—8 a.m. on the last day of finals week—they weren't too happy with that!

Results

Given that I was very satisfied with this course in its traditional format I was very interested to see what the feedback from students would be. At least two of the students were taking another class online in the same quarter and they were very dissatisfied with it, so I was a little concerned with how the students would react to the blended format. I asked for feedback during the quarter at two times—the first right after the initial Breeze session, and the second at the conclusion of the design phase of the course.

> "From conversations with colleagues, I knew that it was important that students feel a connection with the faculty member and that they were not 'teaching themselves.'"

Feedback on the Breeze session included:

I liked the Breeze. It's really cool. I like the interactions and so forth. Discussions are always nice to do, especially with that Margaret Holmes Dentist scenario.

Breeze was an interesting experience. I've never had an online experience like that before. Although the session was neat in the fact that it was like working at home (actually, it was), I still think having it in a classroom would be more effective. Though the collaborated ideas all in a chat was excellent in how everyone could type/speak at the same time, I think having what you showed us in a classroom would be even better, in that I find myself expressing through voice to be easier than typing it out. Other than that, I enjoyed the session and would do it again if need be.

I liked the Breeze session and found it very useful. It seemed like there was even greater interaction in the Breeze session than in regular classroom activities. I hope there are more Breeze sessions to come!

I'll be completely honest—I was extremely skeptical about Breeze going into the session. I thought it was, in a way, just making the situation harder by not meeting face-to-face. My mind changed, though, when the class was halfway over and I was comprehending it better than I have been the face-to-face classes because of the increased interaction. I honestly loved the Breeze session, and can't wait until the next one.

The mid-quarter feedback comments were also interesting:

I think this course was a good choice to make into a blended course. I found that the Breeze sessions can be effective, but can also be more of a distraction than a help at times. I thought that your teaching style was effective throughout the ERD section of the course. Unfortunately, I don't do well in self-taught classes. I know that you keep saying that SQL really isn't self-taught, but that's honestly how it's seeming to me. If I could change one thing about the course, I would put more of the SQL classes face-to-face with us using ISQLPlus at our work stations in the classroom.

I like the blended format that we are using for this class, especially through SQL. We are only going to learn the material through practice and by working on our own, we are getting plenty of practice in, and I think it is effective. We are, though, going through SQL quite quickly which worries me especially for exam 3 in SQL.

I kind of like learning SQL on my own, it allows me to go back to sections that were unclear for me personally without slowing other people down. I think the book explains it rather well.

Modifications

I expect to use a blended format for this class when I teach it in the fall. I will be teaching it in a four-hour once-a-week block at night and that is not an effective model for student learning. Some changes that I will make are:

- Use the discussion question of the week to highlight areas of problems. For example, I gave them some SQL code and an error message one week and asked them to explain why the error message was generated and how the code could be fixed

- Incorporate some of the myCourses best practices into my course—more information on the home page, more navigation links, etc.

- Spread the learning out over multiple days. Although the course is only scheduled for one day a week, I will set up a weekly Breeze session at a time convenient to the majority of the class. This will act as a second lecture to reinforce material. It will be recorded for students who cannot attend the synchronous session

Postscript

I have used the blended learning format several times since the quarter described above. At this point, I do not believe that I will use it again. In general, I find students do not put in the extra time needed to learn the material on their own. They do not seem to remember that they are not meeting face-to-face for two hours per week. I expect approximately 4-8 hours per week outside of the classroom. Thus, in a blended format, they are responsible for 6-10 hours per week. When they are in a face-to-face situation they have several interactive projects to complete during any given class period. The out-of-class time is spent doing Access homework (which is predominantly self-taught) and the in-class time is spent reinforcing design concepts and SQL. Because the class time is self-paced, the students have a greater attention span. They also have me as a ready reference for any questions that arise.

Overall, I think that either face-to-face or completely online seems to work better than a blended format. Student expectations of an online course are different from a face-to-face course. They understand that there is a significant element of independent work. The same does not seem to be true of a blended class.

> "The most difficult part about teaching a blended course is getting traditional students to buy into a non-traditional concept—that of doing part of the work independently."

On the positive side, I have learned to use time above and beyond the scheduled class time to reinforce concepts using Connect, the current version of Breeze. Students like this additional time with me to ask questions on confusing topics and generally chat with the class as a whole. They tend to be less inhibited online than they are in the classroom, which allows for a much richer discussion. Additionally, I find that the low-stakes quizzes that I instituted in later blended sessions work well for traditional classes, encouraging students to read the text before coming to class.

As a final postscript, I think that education is changing, as it must. More non-traditional students are attending college and the cost of college is driving many students into the workplace before they can finish their education. There is a definite need for both blended and online courses in this environment. From my perspective, the most difficult part about teaching a blended course is getting traditional students to buy into a non-traditional concept—that of doing part of the work independently. This will come with time, and eventually I believe that students will appreciate the flexibility of the blended course. And when that happens, everyone will benefit.

Pam Neely is an assistant professor in the decisions sciences and management information systems department in the E. Philip Saunders College of Business.

David Pritchard
Global Issues
Management, Marketing and International Business Department
College of Business
2006-2007 fall quarter

Background

I adopted blended learning in order to redesign a four-hour evening course, Global Issues. From weeks three through eight, students used myCourses for a two-fold purpose.

- First, the class teams met online on a weekly basis to discuss and arrive at a written conclusion on topics posted on the team's discussion board. The topics ranged from reading an article to giving an evaluation of guest speakers (in class or online using the Breeze/Connect web conferencing system)

- Secondly, we used the blended learning format for the online team projects with a separate discussion area. I later implemented a blended format in another class, Global Introduction, which was done after I showed these students what upper-level students were doing in the Global Issues course and they wanted the same format

Method

After implementing the blended portion of the class, the meeting time in the classroom went down from four to three hours from Weeks 3 to 9. Because of the heavy use of online discussion (some 1,500 messages were posted during the course), the workload increased for both the students and me. It took the class about two to three weeks to figure out how to effectively post and organize discussions and get comfortable with the online component. While the goal was a virtual team project, students used face-to-face meetings as well as the team discussion boards for developing their team projects.

I did encourage a degree of competition in the posting activity by showing (via the classroom projection system) the students' posting statistics by individuals and teams. This reinforced to them that I was monitoring their posts and that use of the discussion board comprised a significant part of their participation and team grades.

Modifications

- In the future, I will implement the blended team discussion board in Week 1 of the class; it takes the students a few weeks to get a useful benefit out of the process

- I did find "phantom" posting by students stating they were meeting or working on the team projects, when in fact they were not doing so

- I will keep refining the use of the blended format because it makes the class more enjoyable by provoking more and better discussion between team members and others in the class

David Pritchard is an adjunct professor in the management, marketing and international business department in the E. Philip Saunders College of Business.

Todd Mittler
Human Resource Information Systems
School of Hospitality and Service Management
College of Applied Science and Technology
2005-2006 fall quarter

Background

Human Resource Information Systems is an elective course in the Human Resource Development program. The objective of the course is to orient students to the fundamentals of information systems management in the context of the Human Resources business.

I joined the department as an adjunct instructor in the spring quarter of 2002-2003. My initial several quarters were a learning experience, as I worked to improve course content and its delivery. Although the course was received positively by the students, there was one overwhelming aspect that needed improvement—the class was simply not as dynamic as I hoped. I found it challenging to stimulate active dialogue in the classroom. Also, asking open-ended leading questions to get the students to relate their academic knowledge or professional experiences to our course concepts was only moderately effective. Finally, I found that the professional (working) students were more active, while students that came straight from an undergraduate program were more passive in the classroom.

Objectives

After meeting with Online Learning staff, we established two primary goals for blending the course:

1. Reduce actual classroom time by 50 percent and reallocate remaining contact hours to online activities
2. Increase student participation, dialogue, and interaction

Method

The first part of the development process was to learn about the blended learning model—the objectives, methodology and the resources/tools that are available to faculty. In my initial meeting with Online Learning, we reviewed several existing blended courses and started brainstorming areas where we could incorporate blended learning techniques.

First, I set out to analyze the existing course at a higher level. I developed a planning matrix to organize course components such as weekly sessions, assignments, projects, assessments and participation criteria. Various blended learning techniques and courseware functionality were identified and placed in a separate dimension. At the intersections, I detailed how the course components could be delivered using blended learning techniques. This activity proved to be valuable in the breakdown of tasks for myCourses development related to discussions, individual and group work.

"Weekly online pre-class discussions were effective in increasing participation levels in the classroom. The pre-reading and online discussion stimulated the students to consider the course concepts and how they could be applied."

Then I established a weekly schedule. The beginning of the week was focused on preparing the students for Thursday's classroom session. Pre-readings from our text would be assigned and online discussions would relate to the reading. The objective was that the early week activities would get the students thinking about the weekly topic and allow them to share their thoughts and experiences.

In the Thursday class, we would re-engage some of the prior online discussion points, talk about the weekly topic and then proceed to the lecture, which would expand upon the weekly topic. The students would leave class with assignments and readings for the next week, to be completed over the remaining days of the week.

Content

Content modules were configured for general course information and for weekly topics. The weekly modules were structured so that each week had content on overview, resources and assignments. The overview served to orient the students to the weekly topics. The resources included PowerPoint files, articles uploaded to myCourses and other information available over the Internet. Additional content modules were setup to deliver content related to Projects, Course Tools and Technology References.

Online Learning recommended that I consider using a tool in class called a mindmap. A mindmap is a pictorial representation of how a central concept is linked to related concepts. Mindmaps provide a good workspace for organizing concepts and presenting them in an easy to understand form. A software application called *Freemind* was used to author our mindmap. *Freemind* is available for free under GPL (GNU General Public License); therefore students could download and use the application if they wished.

The notion of the HR Portal served as our central concept of the mindmap. The intent of the mindmap was to incrementally build upon the concept of the HR Portal as we progressed through weekly topics. Each of the HR processes that we covered through the quarter branched out to detail the software features, the data to be managed, as well as implementation considerations. After each class the updated mindmap was available in myCourses.

Course home page

The course homepage was configured to present announcements, the course events calendar, and myCourses reference material. Additional custom widgets were created for online resources and Internet feeds of ERP and HR news.

Discussions

Online discussions were setup to categorize different forums and topics within them. A general forum was used for miscellaneous discussions or questions. Weekly forums, one for each week, were used for pre-class, post-class and assignment discussions. The project forum contained topics for the individual and group projects throughout the quarter.

Gradebook

The gradebook was configured with sections for participation, assignments, projects and tests. Participation was evaluated on a week-by-week basis and was based on activity in the weekly online discussions and contributions to in-class discussion.

Dropbox

The dropbox was setup for students to submit their assignments, projects and tests. The dropbox items were associated to individual gradebook items. This allowed me to review submissions, provide feedback and record a grade without having to navigate between the gradebook and the dropbox sections of myCourses.

Surveys

I created a survey to query the students in Week 1. The objective of the survey was to collect demographics on the students in the class, such as professional experience, student status and experience with some of the applications we would be using in class (Access, Excel, MS Project). It was useful to have students take the survey and then immediately be able to view the results in a graphical format.

Results

There were some successes and challenges with the blended learning course delivery, but overall it was a very positive experience.

The weekly online pre-class discussions were effective in increasing participation levels in the classroom. The pre-reading and online discussion stimulated the students to consider the course concepts and how they could be applied. Students also shared their own experiences, which provided some additional context.

> "The results of this approach were remarkable. The pre-class discussions really got the wheels spinning in the minds of the students."

As a starting point for each class, we would jointly build onto our HR Portal mindmap while reviewing some of the important ideas brought forth from the pre-class discussions. The results of this approach were remarkable! The pre-class discussions really got the wheels spinning in the minds of the students. The first hour of class was typically a flurry of dialogue, as the class brainstormed the critical data, application features and usage considerations (relating to our focus areas). As the instructor, I guided the discussion and edited the mindmap as the class presented ideas. Following the mindmap exercise, I delivered the weekly lecture that expanded upon the weekly topic.

I believe that the goals set forth in the beginning of the project were primarily accomplished. I was satisfied with the increased levels of participation as evidenced by the interactions through online discussions and by the in-class dialogue as we built upon the HR Portal mindmap. I did find, however, that class time was not quite reduced by 50 percent. There a few weeks where the classroom session went longer than intended.

Challenges

One of the practices recommended by Online Learning was a peer review of assignments. Students would exchange assignments with each other and provide feedback before submitting their final assignment to the respective dropbox in myCourses. I provided the students with supporting documents in myCourses about the peer review process. Students reported that the logistics of performing the peer review were difficult to accomplish. They could not exchange, review, provide feedback and edit their assignments in a time frame that would allow them to submit their assignments on time. After a few weeks we abandoned this activity.

Another challenge came with the Week 3 pre-class discussions. The Week 3 pre-class discussions were very sparse, compared to the previous weeks. I contended with this low level of participation by reviewing the intent of the pre-class discussions and the expectations of the students. I also reminded the class that participation in discussions is reflected in their weekly participation grades. This appeared to be effective as participation levels in the discussions were satisfactory for the remainder of the quarter.

Modifications

The development process for blended learning has an ongoing continuous improvement component. There are several things that I am interested in focusing on for the next quarter:

- Digitization of rich media content. There are product demonstrations, for example, that can be recorded and close-captioned. This work will require some Online Learning resources and will need to be scheduled well in advance of the course

- Investigation of how dynamic mindmaps could be delivered through myCourses. This past quarter I had to store static HTML and JPG formats of the mindmaps in myCourses. Freemind has the capability of rendering its native file format within the browser. This feature allows users to view and navigate (expand and collapse branches) around the mindmap without the requirement of having the Freemind client application installed on the computer. This capability will contribute towards an easier way for students to view mindmaps

- Consultation with Online Learning and/or other professors in the Human Resource Development Program to address the challenge I encountered with peer review of assignments. By learning about the successful approaches of others, I will consider revising my own approach and attempting this activity in the future quarters

Conclusions

The experience of redeveloping Human Resource Information Systems for blended learning has provided many benefits. The most important benefit is that the blended learning model has made me a better instructor. Since I am a technologist by trade and relatively new to teaching, the conversion process educated me in some important techniques to elicit the level of student participation that was missing in the course.

myCourses provides a great framework for executing blended learning techniques. The features enable instructors to deliver collaborative and individual learning activities. The online activities allowed students to consume basic course content and encouraged them to start applying concepts prior to the classroom time. Consequently, the time in the classroom was certainly more dynamic and permitted us to clarify and expand upon more complex concepts.

Postscript

I taught this course in the blended format until 2006-2007 fall quarter. Although I am not currently teaching a course at RIT, I am still involved with Learning Technology Programs at Wegmans. Also, as a manager I try to bring blended and just-in-time learning and training to my staff so we can meet our business objectives and/or job responsibilities.

Todd Mittler is an adjunct instructor in the human resources development program, School of Hospitality and Service Management, in the College of Applied Science and Technology.

Ian Mortimer
Internet Marketing
Marketing, Management and International Business Department
College of Business
2007-2008 winter quarter

Objectives

The winter quarter of 2007-2008 was my second experience teaching at RIT. In winter quarter 2006-2007, I taught Internet Marketing as a classroom-based course in a four-hour block on Thursday evenings. In addition to the opportunities that I have teaching at RIT, I teach graduate students at St. Bonaventure University in a similar class.

My primary motivation for teaching a blended course was a demanding travel schedule—the flexibility of the blended format was advantageous. However, upon reflecting on it, I really like the blended structure, and I feel it is beneficial for both students and faculty: students get the benefits of working on the class when it fits into their busy schedules; faculty can more easily track the learning that is occurring (or not occurring).

Method

I believe there are three aspects of my class worth highlighting for future considerations of blended learning:

1. Lessons learned from the "learning week" strategy

2. The strong correlation between classroom participation and online participation

3. The application of blogs in the experience

The "learning week" strategy

Before the start of the quarter, I worked with the Online Learning department on strategies to transition my previous syllabus to the blended environment. The department's instructional designers were very helpful in providing pointers and recommendations on how to manage student expectations with blended learning, and how to build a model that would make sense.

When I left my training with Online Learning, I had, in hand, a delivery strategy called the "Learning Week." The learning or instructional week is designed to ensure that although we would only be meeting on Monday evenings, there is documented guidance and expectations to help the student learn independently. My learning week was as follows:

Thursday: I would post the discussion questions to the two case studies that we would cover that week.

Friday - Sunday: Students read the case studies and contribute to the discussion threads in myCourses.

Monday: Class is held from 4-5:50 p.m. The typical agenda would be to have an hour-long lecture on material relevant to our learning objectives and case studies. Also, we would spend approximately 30 minutes reviewing the cases in more detail and highlighting the best contributions. Towards the end of the term, we spent a lot of time going over the final projects and book assignments.

*Tuesday***:** In addition to the case studies, students were responsible for reading and making postings on a blog they created. The blog was their evidence that they read the books and analyzed the material. Also, they asked questions on their blog that I would follow-up on.

Wednesday: Blog postings were due for review.

From an instructor's perspective, the learning week was exactly what I needed to frame my expectations for the students. However, from the students' perspective, it was initially difficult for them to get their heads around it. We spent quite a bit of time the first few weeks going over the expectations and, for some unknown reason, it was problematic for some of them to understand. In addition, when we had to make adjustments in the agenda and deliverables for a given set of weeks, and the learning weeks were adjusted, it caused some of the students to get anxious.

Moving forward, I will continue to use the learning week format. However, I need to find a better way of keeping the students on track from week to week, and make the expectations easier to understand and more transparent. For the students who are last-minute procrastinators, the learning week went against their traditional learning process; they had to budget time to keep on track and it is less forgiving if you fall behind. For those that manage their time well, they did fine.

> *'I really like the blended structure, and I feel it is beneficial for both students and faculty: students get the benefits of working on the class when it fits into their busy schedules; faculty can more easily track the learning that is occurring.'*

Online participation

An item that I paid close attention to, throughout the learning weeks, was the contributions students made to the discussion threads. I was very impressed with the interaction, the quality of the thoughts, and the insightful postings of the class. Moreover, the online experience was sometimes more interactive than our face-to-face time. Another interesting observation was the strong correlation between student interactions face-to-face and online: the students that excelled in the class also excelled in the discussion threads.

Blogs

As mentioned, each student was responsible for keeping a blog that reflected their musings and questions on the readings that were assigned. Not only did it have value in requiring students to use a second online medium for their reflections (this is Internet marketing, right?), but it was easy to see the students that spent time and effort compared to those that did not. Without the blogs, I would imagine a smaller percentage of the students would have read the books.

As a courseware recommendation, it would be great to have a blogging component in myCourses. Although there is value in having the students use freeware such as Wordpress and Blogspot, keeping track of all the URLs was a bit problematic.

Conclusion

As mentioned previously, I like the blended format for learning and teaching. Some lessons learned for next year:

- Get content online a lot earlier: at times, I felt I was a bit last minute in getting the right information in myCourses.

- Incorporate chat into the content areas: I didn't use this part of myCourses, but I will use it for some of the Q-and-A on deliverables (e.g. Ian will be online from 8-10 p.m. in the chat area to address any questions on final projects, etc).

- I required the class to write a two-page summary just before the holiday break. Next year, I am going to use the online quiz functionality as a gauge to monitor progress—possibly every third week. However, by having the students do case write-ups and papers (this quarter), it exposed some of their poor writing skills. Although not a learning objective, we did spend time reviewing some basic grammar and effective writing.

All in all, it was a great experience, and I look forward to next teaching the course again.

Postscript

Based on the positive experience I had teaching Internet Marketing in a blended format, I have been assigned Principles of Marketing for the fall 2008 quarter in a blended format.

"An interesting observation was the strong correlation between student interactions face-to-face and online: the students that excelled in the class also excelled in the discussion threads."

I am interested in learning if there is a difference in engagement levels between a more advanced elective (Internet Marketing) and the survey course for marketing (Principles of Marketing). Because of the nature of the course, I will be using a formal academic textbook in lieu of the business literature and case studies I used for Internet Marketing. Although the textbook does come bundled with many teaching support mediums (DVD, discussion suggestions, etc.), it will be interesting to see if students are as inspired to engage on academic and theoretical topics as they were on the case study scenarios.

In lieu of handing in papers, I will continue to use blogs as a way for students to express their ideas, questions and insights. I find this medium is very helpful given the structure of the class.

In addition to teaching marketing at RIT, I work for a firm that specializes in student engagement and retention. Our "Success Coaching" model is premised on the fact that students are more successful and happier when there is a higher level of engagement in the community (both academic and non-academic), and our coaching staff drives them to optimize their experience. As a firm, we infuse structure and support into the college experience.

It is interesting to note that as students are afforded the opportunity to learn and engage in a class on their own time—through blended learning or completely online instruction—providing additional support and guidance in time management, setting goals and milestones, offsetting personal or social challenges through counseling and coaching, etc., becomes even more important. It would be an interesting study to try and correlate life management capabilities with blended learning satisfaction and outcomes to see if there is a correlation.

In thinking back to last winter quarter, anecdotally, the students who were on top of things—or at least perceived to be—thrived. This may be true in any learning environment, but I would hypothesize that students who are intellectually gifted can mask lack of life management skills more easily if they are face-to-face with instructors. In a blended environment, proof of knowledge and capabilities are more on the responsibility of the student through focused asynchronous learning.

Ian Mortimer is an adjunct professor of marketing in the marketing, management and international business department in the E. Philip Saunders College of Business.

Patricia Wollan

Management of Financial Institutions
Department of Accounting and Finance
College of Business
2004-2005 spring quarter

Summary

During the spring quarter of the 2004-2005 academic year, I used a blended format for my Management of Financial Institutions class. The course objective is to examine different types of financial institutions—such as commercial banks, savings banks, insurance companies, pension funds, etc. A major focus of the course is to identify the various risks these institutions face and to examine the tools used to measure and manage these risks.

This course typically meets just once a week for four hours. Clearly, it would be inefficient to lecture for four hours straight. I would be exhausted and the students would be bored and unreceptive. Therefore, to put more emphasis on active learning, I have incorporated a bank simulation game—the Stanford Bank Game—as a major component of the class.

With the Stanford Bank Game, students get hands-on experience in how to manage a commercial bank. As its name suggests, the simulation allows students to make all necessary decisions about products, interest rates, credit policies, etc., to run a large commercial bank. Groups of four or five students run a bank. Each student takes on an executive role such as VP for Commercial and Retail Loans or Bank Economist. The student teams then run their bank for a year and a half (i.e. six quarters). In each of six weeks, they make decisions for the bank's next quarter. When these decisions are input into the simulator, it generates an 11-page report. The report provides the bank's financial statements, portfolio breakdowns and analysis, economic and statistical information and competitive data. The students use the information in this report to assess their prior period decisions and to make their decisions for the next period.

Much of the work for the simulation is self-directed. Each student is given a 100-page user manual for the game, along with written suggestions for how they should evaluate their specific area of the bank. I posted these materials in RIT's myCourses course management system for ready reference.

Objective

Prior to the spring quarter of the 2004-2005 academic year, I had used the Stanford Bank Game for the Management of Financial Institutions class in two prior quarters. In these prior sessions, I had expected the students to set up their own analyses and to coordinate their efforts outside of class. While the second class offered a better learning experience than the first, it was clear to me that, for substantial improvements, students would need a lot more structure, monitoring and assistance from me as they completed their individual tasks. In addition, they needed a way to keep in touch with each other without having to physically meet as a group. The optimal solution was to set up this class in a blended format and assign students to online discussion groups.

Method

Under the blended format, much of the individual work for the bank simulation was completed on myCourses. For each bank, I set up an online discussion area for each of the six banking quarters. To get each bank started, I uploaded a large, multi-worksheet spreadsheet. This master spreadsheet was then used for all of subsequent analysis and it contained all quarterly decisions made by the bank. During the course of a week, each "bank executive" completed an analysis related to their area of bank operations. This work was completed asynchronously using myCourses discussions. One by one, students downloaded the master spreadsheet, made their updates and then uploaded the next version of the spreadsheet. As chairman of the board for each of the banks, I responded to the executives' questions, monitored their progress and pointed out errors and made suggestions for improvement.

The deadline for all spreadsheet entries for a given quarter was midnight on the Saturday before class (which was on Monday nights). However, some entries had to be made earlier in the week because they were needed as inputs for additional analysis.

Final decisions for each quarter were made during a one-hour executive committee meeting held during class time. These meetings were scheduled in the computer lab so that the bank executives had access to their bank's master spreadsheet.

Results

Overall, I feel the blended format was an improvement over the 100 percent in-class alternative. Since I could see what the students were doing in their online groups, I was able to give them feedback, assistance and advice as needed. As a result, students were able to get up to speed with their given area of the bank much more quickly than their counterparts had in prior quarters.

The first time that I used the Bank Simulation Game in this class (in a classroom-based course), I did not require the students to use the discussion boards on myCourses. As a result, their work was uncoordinated, inefficient and, in many instances, incomplete. The in-class group sessions were much longer than they were in the blended format but they were not a particularly valuable learning experience. I spent my time rushing from group to group, helping the students get up to speed with the basic analysis. Little time was spent developing strategy or sharing what had been learned in each functional area. Through the blended format, it became possible to assist students with their weekly analysis before class. With the basic analysis complete, students were able to learn a lot more in their weekly in-class meetings.

> "Since I could see what the students were doing in their online groups, I was able to give them feedback, assistance and advice as needed. As a result, students were able to get up to speed with their given area of the bank much more quickly than their counterparts had in prior quarters."

Modifications

One aspect of the course design that was flawed was the allocation of in-class time. I simply sliced one hour from each of our class meetings to compensate for the time the students and I would spend interacting via the discussion board. In retrospect, I think this was a mistake. It would have been better to keep the in-class time at four hours for the first three weeks while the students were learning about the simulation. That way, I could have increased the computer lab sessions to two hours. During these sessions, I could have helped the students to get a better understanding of their roles before expecting them to complete their weekly analysis on their own. Fairly rudimentary exercises such as asking students to block out the cells they were responsible for within the master spreadsheet would have helped them to get to know their way around the spreadsheet and give them a color-coded guide for their first few inputs.

Postscript

For the two years after first offering this course in the blended format, I continued to refine and improve the course—more time was spent in class supporting and preparing for the work that would be completed online during the week. As noted earlier, the purpose of the course design was to make the course more applied and focused on active learning. I feel this objective was achieved. It took quite a lot of time to refine the original design but overall I feel it was a good learning experience both for me and my students. In the last couple of years I taught the course (2006-2007), it was very well received.

One problem with the course in its original form was that it was extremely labor intensive for the instructor during the first few weeks of class as they helped the students get up to speed with their individual roles. As a result, the course has now been set up as the second in a two-course sequence. In the first course, students are given broad exposure to both institutions and markets. In the second course, they build on their institutional knowledge with an applied class that includes the bank simulation that lends itself to the blended learning teaching format.

I am no longer teaching the course since we identified an adjunct professor with a wealth of experience in the banking sector for whom the course was a good fit. However, I did share all of my files and notes with him so that he could start with a beta-tested class design.

In retrospect, I am glad that I designed and taught a class using the blended format. Becoming familiar with the functionality of myCourses and the asynchronous approach to teaching has been beneficial for all my classes. Using online discussion boards provides an excellent way to develop and assess teamwork skills and also provides a good way to get to know students who are not so comfortable speaking up in class.

Patricia Wollan is a lecturer in the accounting and finance department in the E. Philip Saunders College of Business.

John Striebich

Microeconomics
Accounting and Finance Department
College of Business
2006-2007 spring quarter

Overview

I have had some experience in developing and instructing online courses through RIT and the State University of New York system, and also have 15 years of experience teaching college-level (undergraduate and graduate) courses and corporate training seminars and workshops. While this was my first attempt to use myCourses to offer a blended course, I have used myCourses to post assignments, PowerPoint slides, the course information sheet and answer keys for classroom-based courses. My approach to the blended format was to combine the best of online and classroom instruction to maximize the learning environment, better meet students' diverse learning styles and increase the critical thinking skills of my students.

Method

After reviewing some of the blended course strategies used by faculty in RIT's College of Business, I decided to try a different schedule for my course. Most instructors who offer four-hour, one-session-per-week courses still met every week, but shortened each class and substituted the online component for the decreased class time. Teaching a graduate course populated by a majority of adult students, I decided to meet every other week for the full class time and, on the weeks we didn't meet, provide a rigorous online learning experience.

We met the first week of the quarter to cover the first major component of the course—supply and demand—and discuss the blended portion of the course. I did have a couple of students who expressed their dissatisfaction that the course was blended. They commented that they wanted to be taught and didn't want to have to teach themselves. I also discussed the group presentation assignment that involved a live team presentation at the end of the quarter concerning pricing, which is the major emphasis of the course.

During the classroom time I planned to lecture on the important chapters in the text and do in-class activities that assisted students in grasping the key concepts. I feel that one of my strengths is my lecture style, and have consistently received outstanding student evaluations on my instructional style. (One of the issues that I have with online classes is my inability to recreate my classroom instructional style in the online learning format.) I planned to have six class meetings with four sessions involving classroom instruction, one session for the midterm, and the last session for the team pricing presentations.

The online learning component consisted of studying additional textbook material (especially chapters that were ancillary to the major course objectives), reading outside material, online discussions and written assignments. I planned five online discussion topics that connect the course material to real-world applications and got the students to critically think about the material and its impact/affect on business decisions and their personal situations. The nine written assignments consisted of two-page mini-papers that reinforced the application of the material to business decision-making, using real companies and examples. I also planned to offer an online final exam.

Results

I was surprised how well this course went. The students actively participated in the discussions (20 students in class, averaging 120 responses), provided quality comments and showed critical thinking skills. The written assignments really helped students take the theoretical material and apply it to business problems and situations. I have been able to be more productive in the classroom and more efficiently use classroom time to introduce new material, review some of the major points from the written assignments and discussions and answer any questions. Most students have been very positive of the blended format, and liked the time allocation of the course. However, some did comment that they believed there was more work involved in this course than a typical classroom-based course. I still have two or three students that did not care for the online component.

Modifications

I will make some minor adjustments when I teach this course again. First, the class will meet in the classroom for the first two sessions of the quarter. One-third of the students missed the first class session where I discussed the course, explained the team pricing presentation, organized teams and discussed the blended portion of the course. In short, I will still allocate the Weeks 3-10 sessions the same way, but meet two consecutive sessions at the beginning of the quarter.

I have asked students to provide comments on the discussion modules. Students really liked the discussion topics, but do not want more discussions (there are five). I still need to stress to students that I grade discussion entries based on quality, not quantity. The written assignments were also well received, though I will clarify the instructions for two assignments to provide the students with better information on what I'm looking for.

I also tracked my time spent on this course to see how efficiently I was utilizing my resources. I estimate that this course required 35 percent more time than a classroom-based course (even taking into account the time that I didn't have to spend in the classroom). This was attributable to my efforts in setting up the course, grading the online assignments and participating in and grading the discussions. The next time I teach this course I will have the development all taken care of (with some minor tinkering) and now have a system to grade the written assignments, which should save some time. I feel that I have met my objectives and am very satisfied that this delivery method has increased the students' knowledge of this subject and their ability to practically apply the material.

"My approach to the blended format was to combine the best of online and classroom instruction to maximize the learning environment, better meet students' diverse learning styles and increase students' critical thinking skills."

Postscript

I've found that most students are very receptive to blended learning, especially students who have careers and are attending college part-time. These students have such busy schedules that they appreciate the ability to do online assignments based on their schedule (with deadlines), and like some self-directed learning. My first experience with blended learning was not as successful as I had hoped because I had a couple of students in class that did not like the concept and weren't willing to experience the blended class before forming their opinion. These students wanted to have all material presented or reiterated in a classroom environment.

The model that I have found most successful is to assign some discussions online that allow the students to apply the material learned in the course to current events in the business world, give tests and assign analytical exercises and mini-papers online.

In an 11-week quarter, I will schedule seven or eight classes where we meet in the classroom to introduce the material, do problems in groups, have team or individual presentations and discuss current issues in the field.

The weeks we don't have a formal class meeting, students will take online tests, work on extensive problems reinforcing the material, work on papers and discuss current topical issues in the online discussion area.

I have found tremendous success—based on student feedback—offering my method of blended learning for summer courses. With business and personal travel and all the personal and social events in the summer, students really enjoy a blended format in the summer courses I've taught.

Many students have stated that it never made sense to them to sit in a class and take an exam when they could take tests online. Since I teach finance, I've always offered open book and notes during in-class exams and these are easily transferable to the online testing format.

Students also like the opportunities to research current events and connect the theory and concepts we're learning in class. With the blended format, I assign more of these assignments and papers than in a classroom-based class.

There are courses I teach that I personally don't think would be successful using a blended format. This decision involves my perceptions and attitudes about the course material and the best means to provide an optimal learning environment for the students, but I am constantly reevaluating my position as I see what other instructors are doing and as I develop new exercises.

John Striebich is an adjunct professor in the accounting and finance E. Philip Saunders College of Business.

Eric Bruening
Principles of Marketing
Management, Marketing and International Business Department
College of Business
2006-2007 spring quarter

Background

When I decided to teach this class as a blended course, it was my first time teaching in the blended format and also the first time I taught Principles of Marketing.

I first heard about the blended course format opportunity in the quarter before the start of the spring classes. It sounded like a perfect opportunity to help achieve my goals for the course:

- Develop personal marketing plans with resume
- Write a marketing plan for an active business
- Develop virtual-team working skills

Since I am not an academic, but rather an industry professional who enjoys teaching, my value-add to the students is passing along to them real-world experiences and skills. It was my goal to use the blended format to introduce these sophomore-level students to the concepts of teams and virtual working environments. Today's businesses have outsourced so many functions, and have expanded to so many geographies, that learning to work collaboratively by leveraging Internet-based communication tools is essential.

Method

I had read a brochure on blended courses and received some e-mail that introduced the blended format. From these communications, I understood a blended course to be a combination of traditional classroom lecture time and online activities. My understanding was that blended courses reduced the number of hours in a traditional classroom lecture setting and replaced those hours with online collaboration and other less-traditional, more Internet-based learning activities.

Since my objectives for this course included exposing the students to a work-like interaction—use of online collaboration in a blended coursework format seemed an excellent opportunity. I saw the discussion forums as a kind of chat room where the students could meet and discuss assigned topics.

Also, a four-hour lecture in the evening can get very tiring for all parties! Especially those of us who already work a full work day before class starts. Shortening the in-class time looked attractive to me—and I suspected it would also appeal to the students.

I received some initial training on myCourses tools from the Online Learning department, learning how to navigate within the courseware and how to take an existing template and import it as a starting point for a new course.

Results

In-class activities

Using the blended format, I had anticipated using the class time to conduct in-class activities that would not work as well in the online format. However, it became evident that there was still a need to use the classroom time to make sure certain elements of the material were communicated. So the balance of time available for the activities was often insufficient. I think a blended course needs to have a very clear understanding of what activities will be used over the quarter—for what objectives—prior to starting.

Discussion forums

The discussions tool is very useful for getting the students onto myCourses and interacting. I attended a lunchtime learning session at Online Learning part way through the quarter which was very helpful. One key learning I took away was about setting expectations for discussions and online assignments.

In my course, students were asked to comment and discuss several articles relating to the course material. Ways to improve this interaction would be for the instructor to:

- Identify specific critical discussion questions for each article
- Set expectation level of academic or business form of the responses

Our discussions were more at a chat level of rigor than a written college assignment level. While this made for some interesting dialog I don't think it forced the students to dig below the first level of application.

The ability to view all discussion threads and reply to any of them is a helpful tool for the instructor. I was able to direct a public or private note to specific students for encouragement or correction and saw an immediate response (and improvement!) from those students.

Conclusion

The blended format was more work than what I have done in the past in a traditional classroom-based course. Part of the extra work was the learning curve on how to best use the tool. However, I think for any future courses that I teach, I will seek to offer them in the blended format.

Better leveraging of the media resources center, planning the end before starting, ensuring all homework and online assignments are productive toward course objectives and setting expectations for online discussions would improve the overall course delivery.

"It was my goal to use the blended format to introduce the concepts of teams and virtual working environments. In today's businesses, learning to work collaboratively by leveraging Internet-based communication tools is essential."

Postscript

Thinking back upon the blended course experience, there are three actions that I would want to take to improve the learning experience:

1. Establish a clearer set of expectations for the students as to what good participation means

2. Balance the total workload more equitably so that the online and off-line are, in total, no greater a level of effort than a traditional format would require

3. Set up the project work as a "virtual" working assignment

Why these changes?

Lack of clear expectations for good participation allows for many students to coast and not use the online forum as an effective substitute for classroom lecture periods. Dialog online will be richer as the quiet students are more apt to find their voice in this medium. However, it must be stressed that active participation with contemplation and rigor are vital to that participation. A grade must be attributed to the online tasks.

I now believe that I added too many extra assignments in an attempt to use the online component. The objectives of the course were met, but focus was diffused and it diluted overall effectiveness.

Finally, I think setting up the project work as a virtual working assignment would better simulate today's corporate environment. I am currently managing an IT project that serves Kodak Marketing clients located in North America, Europe and Asia. The system is being developed and supported by a virtual staff that resides in Dallas, San Francisco, Reno and Bangalore, India. All meetings are held using conference phone and web-based meetings over the Internet. Using online meeting tools, we define requirements, review technical status and even perform much of the training. This is all done without the benefit of face-to-face meetings.

Although face-to-face meetings in marketing are still highly desirable, my belief is that the effectiveness, speed, convenience and reduced cost of virtual meetings have become the preferred operational model in business. Our students are better equipped to succeed in this environment if they sharpen their virtual meeting skills while in the laboratory of an academic setting.

Thus, when I offer this course again, I will change the focus to greatly reduce the in-class lecture period and emphasize the online participation.

Eric Bruening is an adjunct professor in the management, marketing and international business department in the E. Philip Saunders College of Business.

John Ward
Professional Sales Management
Department of Management, Marketing and International Business
College of Business
2006-2007 winter quarter

Background

During the winter quarter of the 2006-07 academic year, I used a blended format for my Professional Sales Management class. This was an undergraduate section and was scheduled to be taught from 6-9:50 p.m., once a week. The course covers the activities, functions, challenges and opportunities of the sales force manager.

I had taught the graduate section of the course the previous summer and felt that the four-hour class segments would not provide the best learning experience. I wanted to find ways to get students more involved in the case discussions. I also wanted to make sure the students were digging into the core material on their own and not just waiting to have it delivered in class.

I attended an introductory workshop on blended learning in the fall and learned, for the first time, about the opportunity to use a combination of online and classroom learning. In previous classes I had used some basic functions of myCourses, but really did not rely on it heavily as part of the overall learning experience.

Objective

To enhance the overall learning experience for students in the Professional Sales Management course by:

- Reducing lecture time in favor of interactive learning experiences

- Encouraging group work outside of class utilizing the discussion group function of myCourses

- Improving student comprehension of text material by including weekly quizzes online

- Getting better insight into student progress through monitoring the online discussion areas

Method

I sent an e-mail to the class two weeks before the session telling them of my intent to use the blended learning format and what it would mean to them. I decided to reduce the basic expectation for class meeting time by 80 minutes. This gave us a full 150 minutes of classroom meeting time each week.

In-class activities

I used class time for those things that were best delivered in a classroom setting:

- Teaching key concepts through lecture and example. This included discussion and questions about these concepts
- Video
- Midterm and final exams
- Discussion of different views teams had for cases assigned online
- Group presentations and class feedback

Online activities

I used the online learning tools for items that fit best with that format:

- Class introductions
- Online quizzes of reading comprehension
- Group discussions of class cases with the deliverable of a group case solution delivered to the myCourses dropbox
- Discussion groups in preparation for class project
- Written, individualized group feedback on case and project work

Each week there were one or two chapters assigned for reading with a quiz due by midnight on Sunday. Students were also expected to get a case solution into the dropbox by midnight Saturday each week. All of these assignments were graded and given written feedback in the discussion area.

Results

Overall I was very pleased with the results. I queried students several times during the quarter about their perspectives and the response was positive. I felt that I was in a much better position to assess group and individual performance.

The teaching time was much better as students were able to stay engaged for the shorter in-class time period. Students stayed alert, participated in discussions and generally seemed to be taking more in.

> "Students were able to stay engaged for the shorter in-class time period. Students stayed alert, participated in discussions and generally seemed to be taking more in."

The time I spent reviewing team work was also much more effective. Instead of quickly bouncing in an out of groups for very short discussions, as I would in the classroom, I was able to really give clear feedback in the online discussion areas. I found that I could really see differences in students' level of engagement based on their participation in the online discussions. This would be impossible to observe, for all groups, in a traditional format.

I had several students say that they appreciated the weekly online quizzes to keep them on track relative to the reading. My sense was that students were much better prepared for class based on this requirement.

As a newcomer, I struggled with several technical aspects of the course. I would expect to improve in this area rapidly. The Online Learning support staff was very helpful when these issues arose.

Conclusion

In summary, I felt the blended format really helped me to deliver a more effective course. I plan to use the blended format when I teach this course again in the summer. I also plan to develop a curriculum for blended learning in my Marketing in a Global Environment course.

Postscript

I continue to teach some of my courses in a blended format. I find blended learning works very well for evening courses. The reasons:

- Class sessions of 3+ hours are not as effective. Using blended learning I can improve the effectiveness of the course by having students do a portion of the work online

- Many students also work and find the asynchronous online portion to fit in well with their schedules

Continued experience

Most students have provided positive feedback. It seems that the biggest downside for some is the increased level of personal responsibility to complete work outside the classroom. Some found it easier to come to class and have it done. But, measured against the goal of providing enhanced learning for the student who does the work, I find this format to meet all expectations.

Key learnings

- It is critical to be very precise and up front with direction for out-of-class assignments. There is little opportunity for real-time adjustments once the class as started

- Basic quizzing is often seen as a low value-added option. I prefer to focus more on online group discussion and analysis

- Most students share more detailed and thoughtful insight in an online environment

- There is no doubt that blended increases total faculty workload. Although there is more time flexibility, the total hours committed are higher

John Ward is a visiting lecturer in the management, marketing and international business department at the E. Philip Saunders College of Business.

Thomas Traub

Project Management
Management, Marketing and International Business Department
College of Business
2006-2007 spring quarter

Background

This course was originally intended to be a general project management course. However, due to the large number of students from the Decision Sciences program that signed up for the class, the general course format had to be modified to match these students' abilities and interests. Hence, a decision was made several weeks before the start of classes to make this a blended course. This was also my first time teaching this course.

Objective

My objective from the start was to have students read the book during the days before class, do online discussions for five days and then, in class, deliver specific summarizing material. Since this was an undergraduate class, the students were not familiar with the basics of project management. The online discussions were the driving force for students to read the book prior to attending class. This worked reasonably well. Students gained the basics and language of project management, which allowed the in-class discussions to bring the material together.

With students reading and discussing the book prior to attending class, the in-class discussions were designed to clear up any misunderstandings, put concepts on a higher level and integrate learning with real-world examples brought to class.

The online discussions were to help teach the students to learn "elevator speech techniques" and understand the importance of online communication in the contemporary workplace.

Method

My blended course design consisted of the following major components:

- I set up myCourses for general course discussions, specific course discussions by chapter, private discussions for each team, and discussion areas for each of the major assignments. The design was to keep discussions organized for the students and myself

- Soliciting feedback and conducing surveys on a weekly basis when first starting is important. As part of the grade for the online portion, a weekly survey was developed and posted. This also helped to steer the students to online materials in myCourses

- I populated the content area of myCourses with all of the materials necessary for the course and organized it for students to easily find

- As part of project management techniques, I established deadlines for surveys, discussions and dropbox requirements. I used the event calendar to keep them informed of deadlines

- The first night of class, the College of Business library liaison from Wallace Library went through the help she provides, including the online reserves we had for this course

My week-to-week postings were designed to draw on the material read and give a lead for the student's postings that should lead to further discussion. Students were advised in class that the online discussions would be graded based on whether it drew from the book material, whether it showed the student had internalized it and stated it in their own words (not just cut and paste from the book) and whether the student influenced in a positive manner the other students and myself.

Students were advised that if a given week's postings, readings and interactions were not of sufficient volume and substance, then we would stay the full class time to make sure the material was adequately covered. I also advised students that my postings were the material they could expect to find on the exams. Also, if a student's postings answered a test question, it would be flagged for them to review prior to the midterm exam.

The online discussions allowed me to schedule two sessions during the quarter for student presentations, where I would normally do lectures. This additional time was given to expanded presentations by the students, which increased the learning experiences of all.

Results

The most important result to me was that the majority of students read the book prior to coming to class and thus could participate in the evening's material! This made the in-class discussions more meaningful. The online discussions got better as time progressed, and my ability to use the right questions to draw students into the discussions also improved.

My ability to engage quiet students improved through online discussions and private e-mails. The two deaf students in the class were more engaged online and thus became more engaged in the classroom. The use of online discussions allows an instructor to engage students in a forum that seems less threatening, over a longer period of time and at a pace where people can think before they respond. This allows students to prepare responses to be more engaging and not worry about reactions to in-class comments that are quick and off the cuff.

"The majority of students read the book prior to coming to class and could participate in the evening's material. This made the in-class discussions more meaningful."

The online discussions also allowed me to bring in additional real-world discussions that were relevant to the material being studied, versus during just the time allotted in the classroom. These discussions allowed me to better connect with the students who wanted to connect. Nevertheless, I still had a few students who did not want to connect, and were not fully engaged in their education.

Conclusions

In my opinion, students should be offered the choice of taking at least one blended course per quarter. The online discussion component of most blended courses is a critical tool in the success of students in the workplace. Contemporary business is all about marketing / influencing continuous improvement in the organization, and blended learning helps to develop these skills.

The ideas learned in innovative projects such as blended learning, and the continued dissemination of these ideas, is key to RIT having a competitive advantage. I will continue to use blended techniques in my RIT courses.

Postscript

Although I have not had an opportunity to teach a blended course again due to low enrollment of the latest course, I offer these thoughts:

- Class participation—this has always been somewhat subjective to give out grades for and hard to keep records of. The blended format allows more participation by all students and a better way for the instructor to grade

- The communications required in the blended course also "pulls" the instructor to a higher level in the communications to and with students

- Additional communication in written form gives international students additional work in English and also helps deaf and hard-of-hearing students. Monitoring and reviewing online discussion threads helps the instructor to quickly see if a student understands the concepts and is reading the material

- Yes, it was a lot more work on the instructor the first time—maybe 50 percent more. I am sure this will go down as the learning curve kicks in. However, it allowed me to spend more time on a subject—on my schedule

- Blended courses in combination with myCourses are effective tools for education and communications to students

Thomas Traub is an adjunct professor in the management, marketing and international business department in the E. Philip Saunders College of Business.

John Farrar
Sales Management
Management, Marketing and International Business Department
College of Business
2005-2006 spring quarter

Objective

The objectives in teaching Sales Management in a blended learning format were several:

- Help the students learn the material

- Help them to apply that learning

- Create more of a facilitated learning environment

- Engage the students more and thus provide a more interactive classroom environment

- Reduce the length of the straight classroom time of almost four hours to "some" shorter time, but make that time more productive through pre-work

- Use online quizzes to help students identify those areas that they need to review

- Create a dialogue outside of the classroom between students and students and students and professor on topics covered in class

Part of my interest also came from observing my two oldest children who, as homeschooled students, were taking online AP courses. Quizzes and discussion groups were a part of their instruction and I thought that, if it could be combined with classroom time, it would be a highly effective learning process. It would take learning from a purely directed process to one of facilitated learning.

Method

Students were advised that part of their grade would be based on their participation in weekly threaded discussions and quizzes. The discussions would be based on materials that were going to be covered in the next class, or on materials that had just been reviewed in the previous class. In either case, the goal was to engage the students each week outside the classroom through discussion forums to make them think and explore a critical issue.

Both the quizzes and discussion groups would provide them with instant feedback, either from me or from other students. The discussion topics and quiz results could then be used as a springboard in the classroom for a more interactive experience.

The discussion board and quizzes were graded based on participation and not on content (that was left to homework and exams). The exception to this would be if a student's final grade fell on the borderline between grades, the quality of their discussions and quizzes would then be the determining factor for their final grade. Grading was based on the percentage of the discussions and percentage of quizzes that the student completed. This percentage was combined with class attendance and class participation (involvement) to make up the student's class participation grade, which represented 20 percent of their overall grade.

Results

Overall I was both satisfied and frustrated by my first use of this format. My satisfaction came from the fact that those who did participate were more willing to ask questions, challenge me and generally participate in the classroom discussions. This class was much more involved and we had more of a two-way dialogue and less of a lecture format than in the past. I also often had students stay after class to ask questions about the material or discuss their own experiences.

The frustration came from those students who only periodically participated in the online portion of the course. Not only did they simply occupy a seat in class (unless I directly asked them a question) but their graded materials seem to reflect their lack of participation.

Modifications

Although adding the blended component to the class created increased preparation time on my part, I was encouraged by the potential of the format. I believe that students like to learn through several different mediums, particularly in today's day and age, and respond well to the instant feedback nature of online learning.

I thought the discussion forums provide a tremendous opportunity to have students pre-read materials for class, therefore making class more productive. They also provide an excellent platform to introduce material other than the text into the learning experience.

In order to encourage not only participation, but a higher level of participation, it would be my intent to provide a qualitative grade to the discussion forums in addition to a participative grade. In addition, I would like to provide some sort of grading based not just on the posting of point-of-view to a discussion topic, but also based on responses to other students' comments.

"This class was much more involved and we had more of a two-way dialogue and less of a lecture format than in the past."

Postscript

As an adjunct professor, I do not teach a course each semester. When I do, I make use of the blended learning option since I believe that it helps to keep students engaged. This past semester, the course I taught did not lend itself to this approach as it was more of an experiential learning course requiring the students to conduct field research for a selection of small/new businesses.

I am firm believer in blended learning (even though many students think it means more work).

John Farrar is an adjunct professor in the management, marketing and international business department in the E. Philip Saunders College of Business.

John Retallack
Self Promotion and Business
Photographic Arts Division
College of Imaging Arts and Sciences
2004-2005 winter quarter

Background
This is a course in marketing and general business issues for photography majors. It is a third- and fourth-year elective. Normally, I teach this course once per year, usually in the winter or spring quarter. I wrote the course and have been teaching it for at least 10 years. It has had excellent enrollment statistics usually running with 16 to 20 students.

Objective
My normal syllabus includes:

- At least one class field trip to a photographer's studio here in Rochester

- A long-distance phone call to a working photographer or other individual in the media business (with a conference phone in the classroom)

- Creation of a logo, business card and letterhead

- Four to six student-promotion projects in which students construct mailers similar to postcards or greeting cards with one or more photographs

- Construction of a website

- A number of lectures on contemporary photography business practices

I teach this course not because I have a love for teaching business. However, in my career as a photographer and as a teacher I have known a significant number of very talented (artistic) photographers who have given up and found some other employment because of a complete lack of business skills.

Method
Conference phone calls were replaced by synchronous chat experiences with two recent graduates. The subjects they talked about were the steps they

were taking to establish their businesses. Almost always in the classroom with the conference call I had to prime and push the students to get anyone to talk. Often there were only a few talking. This was not a problem in the chat room.

In place of several illustrated lectures, students were given assignments to research specific marketing projects and report on them in the discussion area of myCourses. These included:

- Award winning promotions published online by *Photo District News* (trade journal)
- An article and website by a photographer's marketing consultant
- A photographer's promotion posted on my courses
- Students posted their website URLs on myCourses for other students to review

Online activities
myCourses was used for:

- Chat with recent graduate Jana Cruder about starting her business in Los Angeles
- Discussion of the posted promotion and other general topics
- Discussion of website creation and general course topics
- Chat with recent graduate Ben Peterson about starting out in New York City

In-class activities
Classroom meetings were used for:

- Critiques of the four promotion projects
- Viewing of selected photographers' websites
- Students showing their preliminary websites for discussion and suggestions
- Lectures on various subjects
- Demonstration of image preparation techniques in PhotoShop specifically for the web
- Lecture on copyright specific to photography

Results
There were several major positive experiences from the blended learning course:

- The chat room experience with graduates was contemporary to the minute and positive. Students' interest was captured—they found it extremely beneficial

- The chat room experience in which basic website creation was discussed; not a how-to, it was a positive example of peer-to-peer support and encouragement

- The chat room discussion of the posted photographer's promotion

- The online discussion area reviews of the promotion awards at *Photo District News*

- The online discussion area reviews of the photographers' consultant's website contents

- In my exit interviews, the majority of students made positive comments

Modifications
A smaller class size will be more manageable in the chat room. Fifteen are enrolled next quarter; there were 23 in this class.

- I posted several items to the myCourses discussion area in which there was no interest. I'll try different kinds of questions next time

- More research projects

- Enforce participation more stringently

Postscript
My blended experience was positive. It was especially valuable to have guidance from Online Learning and reassuring to know that support was available, if needed.

Since that first blended class, I have introduced various blended experiences into my classroom:

- Last quarter, I had students read and respond to an article that I posted on myCourses. It was simple and successful

- In the past, I have used telephone conference calls with industry experts. Doing this through chat in myCourses accomplishes a similar goal but seems to get more response from students and leaves a record that can be re-experienced

John Retallack is an assistant professor in the School of Photographic Arts and Sciences in the College of Imaging Arts and Sciences.

Communications

Ben Woelk
Effective Technical Communication
Department of Communications
College of Liberal Arts
2007-2008 spring quarter

Objectives

I decided to do this class as a blended course for a number of reasons:

- To provide students with an opportunity to learn and leverage online technologies

- To provide a means for students to work in small groups and provide substantive feedback to each other using a peer evaluation tool

- To reduce the amount of classroom face time while providing somewhat weightier assignments

- To enable me to work as full-time staff and teach eight hours of adjunct classes while maintaining my sanity and not having to work 60 hours weekly on campus

- To transfer pedagogical techniques experienced as a student in six fully online classes to a class that had been traditionally taught as a classroom course

Having worked as a technical communicator for a number of years, I understand the importance of staying abreast of new technologies. As we move to more virtual forms of communication, I believe that having students use these techniques now will better prepare them for future technology-oriented careers. (My class consisted of engineering students from a wide spectrum of disciplines. Two of the students were in civil engineering and may not have found the techniques directly applicable; 17 of the students were in more technologically-oriented disciplines and should be able to make use of virtual communications techniques in their careers.)

Method

This was my first experience teaching this course. Although I did not have existing materials to leverage what I had created, I was able to adapt the sample syllabus and exercises provided by the book publisher to my needs.

I believe we used most of the tools available within myCourses (grading, news, discussion, dropbox, peer evaluation, groups) and also used a number of Internet resources, including online grammar diagnostics tools provided by the textbook publisher, Bedford St. Martins. Most of the assignments and group work was conducted in myCourses.

I gave the final exam through the quiz tool in myCourses, providing a mix of short answer, multiple choice, multiple select, true/false and long answer questions. I provided a two-hour window between the scheduled exam time of 10 a.m. Saturday morning and 2 p.m. Tuesday afternoon. Students were allowed to take the exam "open book."

'As we move to more virtual forms of communication, I believe that having students use these techniques now will better prepare them for future technology-oriented careers.'

I experienced two issues with the exam: I failed to activate the exam (although I had set the time parameters and exam window) and one student, who thought the exam would auto-submit, went to dinner, came home and found the exam had not been submitted. He sent me a note about that issue immediately. I also made use of the e-mail notification feature to be able to grade exams as they were submitted.

Results

I administered a student feedback survey at mid-quarter. From what I read of the results, the majority of the students enjoyed the blended format and found myCourses to be of help. At least one student did not find myCourses to be conducive to their learning style. (I contributed to this angst by providing frequent updates to the course syllabus as I tried to adjust the class assignments to their anticipated needs.) A number of students found the course to be disorganized. I think I assumed that they would check myCourses frequently for updates. I believe many of them had relied on a printed syllabus and being able to better plan their workload.

I adjusted both how rigorously I had been grading the homework assignments and reduced the amount of changes to the syllabus after reading the mid-quarter survey results. I believe this mid-quarter feedback helped me to make the course better.

I suffered a bout of appendicitis at the end of April—towards the end of the quarter. The blended format enabled me to adapt an in-class assignment to discussion groups on short notice. Instead of doing in-class work reviewing presentation techniques, I was able to supply links and use the discussion forum to have them post their reactions and respond to their classmates.

Conclusion

I enjoyed the blended learning experience. For me, the blended course was valuable and fairly easy to implement. When I do the course again, I will increase the use of the discussion groups and make use of new pedagogical techniques, such as "pruning" and summarizing the discussions on a weekly basis. (I set up book discussion groups in another class and was disappointed with the student participation.) I will probably do at least one Adobe Presenter event in order to expose the students to web-based meeting tools. I would like to make use of a course blog if that functionality could be added into myCourses and maybe hold a meeting or two in Second Life.

Ben Woelk is a Communications and Training Specialist in the Information Security Department and adjunct professor in the College of Liberal Arts.

Rudy Pugliese

History of Communication Technologies
Department of Communication
College of Liberal Arts
2004-2005 fall quarter

Objectives

My objectives as an instructor and coordinator of a graduate program are to:

- Promote students' scholarship
- Better utilize class time
- Enhance students' understanding of each other's topics
- Encourage those who are reticent to participate in class discussions
- Allow more students to benefit from more of my attention

One means of promoting students' scholarship and research is to have them present their research to a wider audience, especially at a professional conference. However, having excellent research papers is often not enough for students to qualify. Papers are far more likely to be accepted if they are part of a complete panel (normally comprised of three to five papers) with a unifying theme.

I decided to use blended learning as a means of encouraging students to find topics in the History of Communication Technologies course that would fit a common theme and thus increase their chances of being accepted at the annual conference of the Eastern Communication Association.

Students have often told me that the hardest part of a research paper is choosing the topic. Owing to the 10- or 11-week limitation on completion of the project in an RIT quarter, students must select a topic relatively early to gather enough sources and conduct careful analysis. Unfortunately, the topic has to be decided before the students have the complete benefit of the course's content. Consequently, class discussion about research topics tends to center around suggestions offered by the instructor with students asking what has been done in the past to satisfy the requirement. The discussion, as well as some papers, can result in a reinvention of the wheel.

It appears to be a standard practice for students to work alone and clear the research paper's topic with the instructor in advance. A number of students clear the topic with the instructor via e-mail. They are usually unaware of what topics their classmates are researching and often procrastinate. Normally, students wait until after class to ask about a possible topic, but this is an evening course that meets one per week. Given that we depart at 9 p.m., many don't want to discuss assignments after class—nor do they participate much after 8 p.m. (As someone who graduated from a doctoral program where all courses were four hours long in one sitting, I can report that little is learned beyond the third hour.)

Method

Blended learning allows interaction independently of class time, therefore allowing us to continue the in-class dialogue. Often, students don't respond until they have had some time to allow their ideas to incubate, especially if they are apprehensive of face-to-face discussion. Most times these ideas are hatched outside of the designated class time.

I created an online discussion area in myCourses devoted exclusively to research topics. Although I accounted for nine of the 53 total responses in the discussion, students were encouraged to suggest topics they were considering and to solicit feedback from others. Some suggestions were either too narrow or too broad to suit the 15-page length of the research paper. Given that students aren't often familiar with the amount of research that has been conducting and published on a subject, it falls to the instructor to suggest modifications. Students also received ideas from others about topics that were under consideration as well as those that had met with approval.

Results

I noticed the following behaviors in the online discussion:

- Students encouraged one another and praised each other's topics

- They related their topics to what had been discussed in class

- They suggested and provided additional sources and thanked each other for input

- Some related the topics to their experiences at work

- Some invited comments, critiques and suggestions from other students

- One student suggested a series of questions that were stated as hypotheses, thus suggesting a great deal of forethought as well as a subject for an empirical study (I encouraged him to pursue these questions for his thesis)

I have noticed that international students are less likely to participate in the face-to-face portion of the course, yet our three internationals accounted for 10 of the 53 responses of the 20 students. This is slightly above the average of 2.65 responses per student. I also offered students the opportunity to submit a draft of the assignment for feedback. Two of the three students who took me up on the offer were international students.

One of our students was a civil engineer who specialized in transportation. She was able to tell others how much information there was available on certain topics and issues related to transportation, particularly digital/satellite radio and the transportation industry. Another was interested in "black boxes" used in aviation. A third was interested in black boxes in automobiles, especially since the first court case involving one took place right here in Monroe County. These three students have formed a panel that I have submitted to the Eastern Communication Association. Our department has also asked them to present in our colloquium series.

I doubt that these results would have occurred without blended learning. I intend to continue its use.

Rudy Pugliese is a professor in the communication department in the College of Liberal Arts.

Susan Barnes
Interpersonal Communication
Department of Communication
College of Liberal Arts
2003-2004 winter quarter; 2004-2005 winter quarter

Background

I first taught Interpersonal Communication as a blended course in winter quarter of 2003-2004. Several aspects of the first blended course were highly successful—such as using online quizzes to encourage students to read the textbook and having students introduce each other face-to-face and online.

After reviewing what worked and what did not in the first blended course, the second course was revised and offered winter quarter 2004-2005.

Method

Some of the revisions made to the second course included:

- Developing stronger teacher presence in the online portion of the course

- Posting PowerPoint presentations to myCourses before each face-to-face class

- Using the broadcast function of myCourses to send students e-mail reminders about when projects and assignments were due

I personally broadcast an e-mail message to all the students before the class started to welcome them to the class. This was received very favorably by a number of students and it set the tone for the blended portion of the class.

Results

Discussions

The most successful online assignment in the course was to require each student to write an online introduction and respond to the introductions of two other students.

This was successful for two reasons. First, it enabled shy, deaf and hard-of-hearing students to communicate on more equal ground. Secondly, it provided an opportunity for students to develop their computer-mediated-communication skills.

As a result of sharing information, new friendships formed between students in the course—a topic covered in the coursework of Interpersonal Communication. These introductions were later used in the class in an analysis assignment. However, the students continued to exchange messages with each other after the official assignment had ended. On the positive side, students developed friendships. On the negative side, their discussions became more personal and, after the assignment had been graded, I turned the electronic space over to them to use as a discussion space because of the social nature of the discussions.

> *"The greatest success that I have had with blended learning was the recent course I taught in Second Life. It was an amazing blended experience."*

Groups

I've tried several times to get students to work in groups using the online tools. This aspect of the course has not been as successful. A contributing factor is time management. Students have difficulty managing their time in a blended course, which did become a topic in the class. As I tell students, working together in online groups is a skill they need to learn for future employment.

I have two recommendations to make online groups work better. First, discuss the issue of time management earlier in the course. Second, make group participation a larger part of the grading process. Although students were reminded to participate, grade penalties seem to be the only key motivator in changing student behavior.

Writing

Another issued that I noticed in this course was the increased use of Internet shorthand used in student writing assignments. In an online discussion about the use of Internet shorthand in academic contexts, the students stated that they thought edited American English should be used in *all* academic contexts. But, included in these discussion messages was Internet shorthand—such as acronyms, emoticons and playful spelling. In fact, some of these shortcuts also appeared in the students' submitted paper assignments. Use of Internet shorthand in online learning is a topic worthy of faculty discussion.

Postscript

While the Blended Pilot started in fall 2003, it seems like I have been using blended strategies in the classroom for much longer. Over the years I have had great successes and some failures with blended learning. The biggest failure was when I first tried to introduce public blogs into the classroom. I used software that was available on the Internet. Our blogs were going very well until we got spammed. The spammers figured out how to send messages to the blogs and we were hit so hard and fast that the program crashed. Student names were also being associated with risqué topics! It took me a long time to straighten this mess out.

The greatest success that I have had with blended learning was the recent course I taught in Second Life. We used the fact that Second Life is a commercial site to examine advertising in a virtual world. We had residents from Second Life come into the class and give lectures—of course this was done in the virtual world itself. Students had meetings in Second Life and they explored the environment. It was an amazing blended experience.

Another success was receiving a National Science Foundation Grant to study online learning environments and social networking. There are several preliminary findings that have an impact on blended learning. First, men and woman seem to be balanced in their usage of online systems. In other words, men and women are equalized in these environments. Second, social networking sites—such as Facebook and MySpace—are influencing the ways in which students view online learning systems. This could have important implications for blended learning because students compare these sites to the courseware sites we use in universities. Of course, social networking sites are much more engaging than closed course management systems such as myCourses. In four years, we have gone from engaging students with blended learning to boring them because course-based networks are not as interesting as social networks. We now need to think about how to add more social-networking features to blended courses.

Since I have become involved with blended learning, it has changed the way I teach and my research agenda. Most of my research is on the study of social networking, which has serious implications for blended learning. When I look back to 2003 and think about how the tools for blended learning have advanced, I am excited about the possibilities for the future for both research and teaching.

Susan Barnes is a professor in the communication department in the College of Liberal Arts.

Lisa Hermsen
Science Writing
Department of English
College of Liberal Arts
2004-2005 spring quarter

Objective

The Science Writing class is designed to use quite a bit of multimedia during the first parts of the course. In addition, the class requires quite a bit of independent student writing. At the center of the course, students are required to venture outside of the classroom and find live science in practice at RIT or in Rochester. Once found, the student will spend at least a week, maybe two, interviewing participants and observing the work, in preparation of writing a final document—a real version of science writing. Ideally, the blended application would allow me to conference online and stay closely connected with every student. Once online drafts were turned in, we could begin the revision process. These were the most exciting applications I saw for this course.

Method

For the multimedia aspect of the class, we located good science reading and visuals in the works of Carl Sagan and Brian Greene, both of whom thrill audiences with explanations of cosmos and strings. The class also streamed a Words Matter series from CalTech, in which a group of science writers discuss their craft.

The application of a blended format meant that students could access this multimedia material from myCourses on Wednesdays and also respond to an online discussion prompt. Then, on Mondays, in the classroom, we reviewed their responses as well as introduced new reading. This process was meant to guide students toward defining their own collaborative criteria for what formulates good science writing.

I used the blended application to introduce multimedia into the classroom and students seemed at first to think this was a good application.

Results

While students were dutiful in watching the visual material, they were not so dutiful in responding to the online prompt. I often needed to remind them to complete a response before class time Monday. In addition, I noticed students were responding to the prompt as if they were responding to me. They did not read nor respond to each other's comments. So the online discussion sessions turned into monologues rather than dialogues.

In the classroom discussion of the topic, however, their response was usually active and sometimes heated. I suspect that my prompts were not as suitable to online class discussions as they could have been, and I ought to have taken a closer look at the kinds of prompts other faculty have used. I did manage some discussion, especially in areas about which students were passionate (was Sagan the better science writer, though dated?). And when I really pushed, students read (though did not give much response) to the prompt regarding criteria for science writing. I knew they were reading each others' responses because in the final assignment, most of them used a clearly collaborative set of criteria in their assignments.

As for conferencing, most students went straight to e-mail for conferences. I managed, by the end of the quarter, to get students to use the dropbox in myCourses instead of sending drafts by e-mail (but only by threatening the loss of their documents). Interestingly enough, there were at least three or four students who preferred to conference in person and used the blended time to seek me out in my office.

Conclusion

Finally, then, I do see the possibilities for this pedagogical structuring of a classroom. Students can view material wherever/whenever they are and have access to me as a reader for the "real" science writing paper. They can turn in drafts online and receive my comments online. This process should have improved the writing experience and the final papers. In fact, most of the papers did look pretty good and did go through several drafts. I even suggested publication to one student. But I am not sure the students found the experience very "personal" as writing instruction is usually perceived to be?

Postscript

When I planned to use blended learning pedagogies for this class, I had hoped for a course strategy that would allow me to use a wide variety of multi-media material—especially streamed video from CalTech's WordsMatter series and from a NOVA special with Brian Greene on String Theory—and incorporate those more seamlessly into the class design.

Rather than to use class time to view the media and fit discussion in at the margins, or to require out-of-class viewing and delayed discussion, I believed the blended environment would allow me to use video and online discussion in a more symbiotic relationship. In fact, I think this singular goal was achieved in this course, more so than in versions of the course I've taught thereafter, in which I simply did not use the multi-media materials or attempted, with little success, various other methods of incorporation.

"Which comes first, the creation of a course or the use of an online delivery system like blended learning? Ideally, I suppose, these ought to be symbiotic, so that blended learning is not just a pedagogical add-on."

However, for other aspects of this course—especially assigning formal writing and preparing the final copy—students seemed to thrive with more peer and instructor face-time. That is, while the blended format worked well for daily class work and provided a lot of nice opportunities for informal writing, the formal assignments required more and different time. Students wanted quite a bit of clarification about the rhetorical exegesis of the assignment. They needed to imagine why they were writing, who would be reading and how the writing would be evaluated. We seemed to need more, rather than less, time in the classroom together to come to collaborative understanding of the writing process.

When I first taught the blended class, the class was still new. In fact, it had only been offered and taught twice prior. As I speculate now, I have to wonder whether I would try to experiment with blended learning in a class that was so newly created. I believe this is an important question for the future of blended learning. Which comes first, the creation of a course or the use of an online delivery system like blended learning? Ideally, I suppose, these ought to be symbiotic, so that blended learning is not just a pedagogical add-on. However, now that I've taught the course more often and can work with colleagues who also teach the course, I might be more inclined to go back and re-work a blended environment for the course.

Also, there is the question of providing formal instruction in writing in the blended environment. I do believe that online learning offers students more opportunity to write. But does instruction that incorporates writing differ from instruction that places the process of writing from drafting to editing at the center of instruction? And, if so, how might a blended learning experience help provide writing instruction that goes beyond just practice in writing? How can blended learning be used to teach the professionalism of writing?

I continue to have a lot of questions, and at the moment only imagined answers. I taught a fully online course this summer—a general education writing course. I used a lot of electronic question and answer and weekly journaling as informal writing opportunities—not merely for class discussion, but as steps in the writing process to prompt students as they began to think about their formal writing assignments.

A first try at defining "neuroethics" became a 10-day group effort at building and refining a concise and shared definition. I observed much of the promise regarding collaborative work and informal writing activities that lead strategically to first drafts and final revisions. However, the pacing of a writing course is very important. And I found that modeling the writing process in virtual space took much strategic preparation.

Students in the online course often wanted to "self-pace" and move, due-date by due-date, to its finish rather than to use daily prompts to build drafts and craft careful revisions with elegant prose. I found that it was important to require more peer review and much revision to slow "class time"—so we spent more time in the writing process and less time hurrying toward the final product. After teaching a single online writing course, I am no expert and I, as well as my students, need to learn how to use technology to support a complex writing process from inquiry to first draft, through review and revision, to a thorough edit and final copy.

Lisa Hermsen is an associate professor in the English department in the College of Liberal Arts.

Grant Cos
Speechwriting
Department of Communication
College of Liberal Arts
2004–2005 fall quarter

Objectives

One of my objectives in blending Speechwriting was to get students to converse on concepts and strategies that are part of writing for speech situations (writing public speeches). Half of the course was to be done online, requiring students to discuss and critique aspects of rhetorical theory. Another objective of blending the course was to increase critical interaction between students through written, online discourse and determine how students edited their work to reflect this interaction. Students would have to communicate critically with each other for the purpose of improving their writing.

Method

I equally divided the course into online and classroom components. We spent the first week in a traditional face-to-face setting. The second week had us meeting once a week in the classroom and once online. The online portion of the class consisted in a posted mini-lecture and some question prompts for the students. The questions were posed to initiate a discussion of theory among students.

After the fourth week, the class was broken up into six permanent groups of three students. The instructor served as a "floating" fourth member of each group. The online activities always involved group members reading group drafts and providing criticism of at least one member's speech draft. Students were encouraged to read critically for both form and content. As the instructor, I provided brief, concluding comments on each group's critical round-robin.

Results

My preliminary findings (through word-of-mouth from select students) suggest that students did not respond well to the structure of the class. I believe this was partially my poor structure and partially some students' frustration with myCourses. Many students wanted more instructor feedback, with some students resenting the discussion of theory online. These students thought the class should have a more "pragmatic" function.

Other students were, at times, frustrated with myCourses. Rather than encourage full interaction among the class, some found the discussion function of myCourses to promote a one-way response to a prompt question (rather than giving them the flexibility to discuss). Half way through the quarter, I acknowledged this concern and requested that students post their responses to the prompt questions and not discuss them.

On the positive side, a few students used their online group time quite effectively. These students provided excellent feedback to their group members, with a couple using some innovative editing software that I was not previously familiar with.

Grant Cos is an associate professor of the communication department in the College of Liberal Arts.

Computing and Information Sciences

Kevin Bierre

Access and Accessibility
Information Technology Department
Computing and Information Sciences
2005-2006 winter quarter

Objectives

This course was taught as a team course by me and Catherine Beaton. The course examined the problem of accessibility as it related to the field of computing. Issues covered included: accessibility for disabled people, assistive technologies, the effect of poverty on accessibility (the "digital divide"), restrictions on the use of public machines, and the moral, legal and ethical issues associated with accessibility.

Method

There was a large amount of reading required for the course. We felt that review of this material could be best accomplished through an online discussion format. Students were given reading assignments a week in advance and were expected to respond to the readings by posting substantial comments to the myCourses discussion area we set up for each week.

Readings came from the main text, as well as from other papers, texts and websites the students were directed to access.

We provided feedback the first couple of weeks to stop the "me too" comments that some students were posting. We also explained to students that we expected their comments and opinions, not a dry summary of the material they had read.

In addition to the reading assignments, there was a group project that required some coordination between students. We set up a discussion area where students could post their ideas for group projects. This was used by many students to determine which group they wished to join.

Results

We were very pleased with the number of students who participated in the discussions. On average, the typical student participated in 80 percent of the discussion topics. The few students who failed to do much with the discussions also failed to do many of the more traditional assignments, so it appears that it was not just the online component of the course that they were having trouble completing.

The comments that were generated by the students in the discussions were well thought out and, in many cases, led to rather protracted exchanges. The students got involved with the material and we felt that they really understood the point of the various articles and readings.

Student evaluation feedback on the course was generally positive. There were a couple of objections to the blended format. Some students felt that we could have done more with the discussions online. Others wanted more of the project planning to be handled in the discussion groups.

"We were very pleased with the number of students who participated in the discussions. On average, the typical student participated in 80 percent of the discussion topics"

Modifications

Overall, we were pleased with the way the course went. In the future, I'd like to structure the discussions a bit more. Perhaps posing some leading questions would allow students to have a more directed discussion. However, I'm concerned that this approach would narrow the scope of the discussion and possibly eliminate some of the interesting side topics that came up.

I'd like to make parts of the project more visible to the class. Having each group post their design information online earlier in the course could allow the other students and instructors an opportunity to comment earlier in the process.

Conclusion

Based on the feedback from the students and the level of work they submitted, I feel that the blended approach worked well for this course and I plan to continue this approach when the course is run again.

Kevin Bierre is an associate professor in the information technology department in the B. Thomas Golisano College of Computing and Information Sciences.

Sharon Mason
Advanced Routing
Networking, Security and Systems Administration Department
College of Computing and Information Sciences
2005-2006 winter quarter

Objectives

I was motivated to offer my Advanced Routing course in the blended format for the following reasons:

- Students in the Networking, Security and Systems Administration department are generally very connected in terms of online communication. I hoped to take advantage of their skills by implementing a stronger online component than is typically part of the curriculum

- I wanted to challenge and motivate students to take some initiative in learning new technologies and in learning how to learn about new technologies rapidly and effectively

- I wanted to provide students with a forum where they would be able to manage their group projects and where I would be able to monitor their progress

Method

Students were expected to complete three assignments in myCourses: online debates, group project management and exams.

For the online debates, students were organized into groups of six. Each group of six was then split into two teams of three and each team argued one side of the debate topic. Several debate topics were posed throughout the quarter and students had approximately 10 days to complete each debate.

Students also used myCourses group discussion forums to manage a group project. While students were required to present the project to the class during our scheduled meeting time, myCourses provided a centralized location (which I was able to monitor) for the group teams to negotiate decisions, post materials and organize documentation.

Students completed both the midterm and final exams online. Multiple choice, true/false and short answer questions were utilized.

Results
Throughout the quarter, there were several high points and low points.

Online debates

While I still believe in the concept of the online debate, students struggled with exactly what was expected of them. Some students participated with articulate and well referenced postings, while others did not participate at all. Regardless of their level of participation, students were looking for a definitive number of required postings in order to determine their grade, and they had a difficult time with the concept of quality versus quantity. The myCourses courseware worked particularly well for grading this assignment because I was able to post feedback to both the groups and the individuals. In the future, I would attempt to better convey to the students my expectations in terms of well thought out postings and responses to the debate forum.

> *"The blended format lends itself very nicely to group project work. Students could communicate and post materials while I was able to monitor each group's progress and provide feedback."*

Group project

The blended format lends itself very nicely to group project work. The courseware management system provided a mechanism for students to communicate and post materials while I was able to monitor each group's progress and provide feedback. The online gradebook provided a way to easily submit a grade for the group as a whole as well as individuals. I will definitely use this again in the future and there is nothing that I would change regarding this assignment.

Online exams

I offered the midterm and final exams online as an experiment. In an attempt to primarily test the online exam format, I used questions from prior quarters' exams. Students were allowed to take the midterm exam using any computer as long as they logged in and completed it during the regularly scheduled class meeting time. After completing the midterm exam, students requested to be able to take the final exam at any point in time during a specified day. I allowed this as part of the Blended Pilot.

Both the midterm and final exam ran smoothly from a technical standpoint. The system graded the true/false and multiple choice questions. I was able to determine if there were any problems with the questions by looking at the results for the class as a whole. I graded the short answer questions online. This was surprisingly quick and easy to do. Feedback can be provided to each student for each question. Grades are immediately visible in the grade book.

The primary problem occurred while I was grading the final exam. Upon noticing several very similar responses to the short-answer questions, I looked further at the technical information reported by the system such as the location, login time and logout time of each test taker. Unfortunately, several students had collaborated on the final exam and were cited for academic dishonesty.

In the future, I would again consider administering the exam online, but may require students to take the exam at the scheduled class meeting time in a computer laboratory. I would also rework some of the questions to better suit the online format.

myCourses

myCourses worked very well for the Advanced Routing course. In the past, student grades, class postings, presentation materials, group project forums and assignment dropboxes were all housed in different locations using a different software program for each. myCourses provided me with a centralized location for all the course materials. I was able to view students' progress throughout the quarter because all my feedback was visible in one centralized location. I will be able to move materials from one course to another from one quarter to another. In the future I will continue to use myCourses regardless of whether or not the course is being run in the blended format.

Conclusion

Despite some minor bumps in the road, I am a strong proponent of the blended format. From the faculty perspective, I believe that with some more experience with what works well and what needs tweaking, the blended format will provide an effective and efficient means to deliver curriculum. From the students' perspective, I believe that with some more experience with the blended format they will feel more comfortable with the expectations and requirements. I look forward to offering another blended course in the near future.

Sharon Mason is an associate professor in the networking security and system administration department in the B. Thomas Golisano College of Computing and Information Sciences.

Michael Lutz
Formal Methods of Specification and Design
Software Engineering Department
College of Computing and Information Sciences
2005-2006 winter quarter

Background

I was introduced to blended learning via a distinct but related project with Online Learning—how to capture the essence of my Formal Methods of Specification and Design course so that it could be taught by a new faculty member during my 2006-07 sabbatical year. In discussing this problem, Online Learning suggested that I consider a blended approach, as much of what I captured in online discussions could form the basis for the record I wanted to pass on.

Initially I was quite skeptical—how could replacing two hours of face-to-face class time with online activities possibly improve the quality of the course for the students? I did see how this would benefit me—or so I thought—as I was under great time pressure given my teaching load and responsibilities as chair of the Academic Senate. Having a couple of unfilled slots in my weekly schedule was enticing, so I agreed to run the Formal Methods course in a blended format.

By the middle of January I was hooked, and I even introduced a somewhat simplified version of blended techniques in my other courses. Along the way, I learned that the flexibility I gained in my schedule was more than offset by the time I spent monitoring, evaluating and contributing to the discussions my students were having. Blended learning is not a free lunch—done rightly it requires the instructor to be continually involved in the online activities. On the other hand, this was one of the most fulfilling experiences I've had as a teacher, and I will use blended learning in the future whenever it is feasible and appropriate.

Objectives

The Formal Methods course is one with the greatest concentration of mathematical rigor in the software engineering curriculum. What is more, this rigor is quite different from that found in traditional engineering—the focus is less on models that provide numerical measures of quality and more on logical models showing the relationships and constraints between software components. While the students have taken two courses in discrete mathematics as preparation, this course is the first one where they have to apply these concepts to software systems. As such, the students must switch from an operational, programmatic view of software to a richer relational view based on logic, set theory and relational algebra. The result is a course that most students find difficult.

For the past two years I've used a tool called Alloy from Massachusetts Institute of Technology which lets students create and analyze models without resorting to low-level proofs. This approach has been a modest success—and certainly better than what I did previously—but students still grumbled about the lack of support materials, and it was obvious that they were doing most of the work on their own outside of class. From my own experience, mathematics is a field where collaborative activity is nearly essential, as the knowledge of a group of students is almost certainly greater than that of any individual.

Finally, as in all software engineering courses, the students worked in teams on a project. In this case, the project was to model the essential aspects of a system with which they were familiar (upon approval by me). What I wanted was a means by which I could track team progress in real-time rather than just twice a week.

In the end, then, I lectured twice a week for the first four weeks of the winter quarter, after which I held class once a week with the other slot available for team work. I used myCourses, especially the discussion forums, as a mechanism to address three key issues:

1. Ensuring students had at least rudimentary familiarity with the material we were about to discuss in class

2. Providing a mechanism for collaborative mastery of "tricky" material

3. Keeping in close contact with the teams as they worked on their projects

Method

I told the class that 15 percent of each individual's grade would be based on participation, both in-class and via the online discussion forums. In the case of the forums, I said that I was looking for one or two significant contributions each week. A significant contribution could be a question related to the text or some aspect of the Alloy tool, an answer to such a question, or a reflection on some aspect of Alloy related to software engineering. About the only contributions that would be insignificant were "me too" responses.

Reading before class

I set up a forum for discussing the text, with a topic for each of the chapters of the text we were covering. I told students that topic contributions were always welcome, but those made before the class in which the chapter was presented would carry much more weight. In this way, students at least perused the material before class, as otherwise they couldn't make a significant contribution. Combined with periodic short quizzes, the discussions ensured that students were reasonably prepared for the in-class lectures. What's more, the questions that arose made it possible for me to tailor my presentations to the most problematic areas—I didn't have to use a shotgun approach that covered everything.

"Blended learning is not a free lunch—done rightly it requires the instructor to be continually involved in the online activities. Yet this was one of the most fulfilling experiences I've had as a teacher."

Discussions of tricky issues

Though I didn't plan it this way, the chapter topics provided a place for students to discuss tricky aspects of Alloy—often the misunderstandings and misconceptions were cleared up by classmates before I had a chance to respond. A few times, it was apparent that the class was going down a blind alley, in which case I could add a note to help nudge them back on the correct path. This was particularly gratifying to me as a teacher, as I could intervene in real-time and ensure that mistakes did not become ingrained. In the end, I set up a forum for general discussions so that issues not fitting any particular chapter could be raised.

Team activities

Software engineering is a team-based discipline, and thus all software engineering courses have at least one team project. One problem instructors always face is how to make the team activities visible, both as a way of assessing individual contributions and to guide teams that are going astray. Based on the success with the chapter forums, I created a team forum with a topic for each team to discuss its project. In addition, I stated that "if it's not on myCourses, it didn't happen," providing an incentive for teams to post meeting agendas and minutes, to ask questions of me related to their project and to discuss issues asynchronously.

This approach exceeded my expectations, for the postings gave me an insight into the team dynamics, the problems and successes, and the overall team psychology that I never saw in the lecture/lab format. What is more, I was able to keep my finger on the pulse of each team continually, rather than once or twice a week. When intervention was required, I was able to redirect the team immediately, which can be critical given the RIT quarter system.

Results

I was pleasantly surprised by the results—despite some initial grumbling, most students were active contributors, often going well beyond the minimal requirements. Once the discussions took off, they became the focus of lively and energetic exchanges from which all (myself included) profited. I was particularly gratified to see the shy students, who rarely participated in the classroom give-and-take, contribute as much to the forums as the more vocal students. My informal discussions lead me to believe the discussion forums are more supportive of those who need time to absorb and reflect on material before contributing their own thoughts.

Finally, the blended learning style made me more effective as a teacher. I was able to guide individuals and teams in real-time, and I could head off problems before teams backed themselves into a corner. In summary, I was able to address the problems that students really had, and that was the most satisfying part of all.

Michael Lutz is a professor of software engineering in the B. Thomas Golisano College of Computing and Information Sciences.

Stephen Jacobs
Interactive Narrative/Writing for Multimedia & New Media Perspectives
Information Technology Department
College of Computing and Information Sciences
2004-2005 winter and spring quarters

Background

This narrative covers two courses: Interactive Narrative/Writing for Multimedia and New Media Perspectives

I have been using online course management software for asynchronous discussion for several years, and doing so is always dependent, to a certain extent, on the group involved. The 2004-2005 Interactive Narrative/Writing for Multimedia class was a challenge in that it served two different groups with two different expectations of the course. This had nothing to do with the blended nature of the course, but rather was an administrative issue within the information technology department.

Briefly, these two course numbers were at one time for a single cross-registered course on Writing for Interactive Media. Last year, the graduate course was developed into a course in writing for computer games. The courses were supposed to be separate courses with separate audiences for the first time this year, with one graduate course offered in the winter and the undergraduate course offered in the spring. Unfortunately, they stayed cross-registered for the winter and we were put in the position of offering some students something different than what they'd signed on for. They were made aware of the changes and two students dropped the course, but the others stayed on.

Method

In my Interactive Narrative/Writing for Multimedia course, I used a course management system for asynchronous discussion, group messaging and peer review of written work. Additionally I had planned to use the Breeze web conferencing application for incorporating a guest lecture later in the quarter, but the lecturer came to town instead. I also added a "progress report" component later in the course for reasons explained below.

In my New Media Perspectives course, I used the myCourses course management system for asynchronous discussion and testing, and a web-conference system (Macromedia Breeze, now Adobe Connect) for real-time online class meetings and guest lecturers.

Results

Since half the class in the Interactive Narrative/Writing for Multimedia course wasn't there originally to focus on games, while much of the course was focused on that, the discussion portion was tricky. The discrepancy between the two audiences was too great and, though they and I did make an effort, I de-emphasized discussion during the second half of the quarter. Normally in a homogeneous course where discussion is lagging, I push the issue with students and generally am able to move things along. I chose not to do so here, but added a weekly progress report to the last weeks of class. This was helpful in keeping the undergraduates (and some of the graduates) focused on making regular progress on the final project.

This year (2008), I had students submit first drafts of their papers to the online discussion conference in established groups of three. Each student acted as a first reviewer for one paper and a second reviewer for another. Having had some of these students before, I designed the groups so that there would be one known good writer in each group of three. The students were to insert comments into the papers using the Microsoft Word track changes tool. Each author was then to revise the paper with the comments of his peers. Overall, I believe I got a better quality of final product from the students. Anecdotal student comments after this exercise indicated that this was a good learning experience for them. Some students actually commended others in class on the quality and depth of their papers and the pleasure they got from reading them, so this is a strategy I will continue to employ in future courses.

Asynchronous discussion

In my New Media Perspectives section, discussion was slow for several reasons. The first was that the freshman were not used to asynchronous discussion, how it works and what the responsibilities were as far as posting to class. The second was the general usability issues of this part of myCourses. The toolset for this part of the package is extremely poor even when compared to FirstClass, for example (and I'm no great fan of FirstClass either). A third issue was that the course was divided into three sections. This made interaction cumbersome as students are either gated out of interacting across disciplines or all three sections worth of students must add all three courses. Tons of administrative hassles resulted. Next year we should have one large section with three large groups moderated by faculty across disciplines (for discussion, assignments and grading) and a second group of three sets by department for grading (only if necessary).

Testing

I had one case of plagiarism in the first quiz. We made the quiz available for the length of one class period and we put the notes from lectures online in myCourses (something that I don't often do in classes I teach alone). Two students submitted fairly identical answers to one of the quiz questions. Their answers had, in fact, been

> "Where the blended = less classroom time formula worked best was in courses with a specific online community focus as all or part of a course."

copied, pasted and modified from one of the lecture slides. When I called them on it, they admitted that they had been chatting online while taking the quiz and come up with the idea of pulling answers out of the slides while they were chatting to each other. They both said that they initially did not consider any of this cheating but, now that I'd caught them, could see that it was.

To combat this, we made the second quiz "open book and web" and much deeper, requiring them to do things like provide their own definition of new media, compare it with two others across the Internet and cite their sources. This would have been harder to plagiarize (and similarly be harder to identify it). As it turned out, the biggest issue this time was students not reading the questions and doing things like forgetting to cite their sources or provide examples.

The "Third Quiz/Final Exam" really wasn't either. Instead we used the testing system as an online form for students to evaluate projects created by other student teams. This worked fairly well.

"Live" online with Breeze

The Breeze web conferencing system is still a bit rough. It's rare that start-up is seamless, there's often a glitch or two, but eventually it gets rolling most of the time. If, on the one hand students, are unfamiliar with asynchronous chat they may be too familiar with IM on the other. They tended to treat guest lecture sessions as combination lecture/open chat session/back channel sessions and the experience was often chaotic, despite faculty attempts to reign the students in. Luckily, our guest lectures took this as youthful enthusiasm vs. rudeness and went with the flow. Even faculty laying down some guidelines after the first session didn't ensure that it didn't happen again.

Postscript

I am still teaching blended courses, with a couple of caveats to that.

Most of my courses, before and after the Blended Pilot, have included online components of homework assignments, discussion groups, peer-review of writing, etc. As a professor teaching primarily multimedia and game design and development courses, much of that comes with the territory.

What was new for me in the Blended Pilot was the attempt to move so much of the course online that it merited swapping that out for a day of face-to-face class time. For some of my courses, like the game writing course, I found that my technical grad students came into college with too narrow a reading and writing background to be able to give up a day of class time. We needed a lot of traditional lecture, Q-and-A and discussion to fill in the holes in their backgrounds. They still did online homework assignments, discussion groups and peer-review of writing.

Where the blended = less classroom time formula worked best was in courses with a specific online community focus as all or part of a course, like the Online Community, Identity and Social Behavior course. Here, giving students additional time to get accustomed to the online communities they were participating in and becoming active members of proved useful enough to diminish in-class time in favor of more online time. It's likely that in the short-term, faculty in non-technical domains that pursue blended coursework will diminish class time to afford students the opportunity to become comfortable with the tools and techniques in an academic setting. Long-term, I think we'll find blended activities becoming part of most courses and standard parts of assignments so that significant use of the techniques we refer to as blended now will become standard to regular classes.

Stephen Jacobs is an associate professor in the information technology department in the B. Thomas Golisano College of Computing and Information Sciences.

Joseph Hennekey
Managing Cyber Threats to Critical Infrastructure Protection
Center for Multidisciplinary Studies
College of Applied Science and Technology
2007–2008 fall quarter

Objective
The initial objectives of the course were to:

- Replace one-third of the classroom sessions by using every third class to conduct an asynchronous discussion over a five-day period

- Manage all assignment instructions, work-product submission and grading through myCourses

- Use classroom sessions as building blocks for the online discussions: laying the foundation in concepts and terminology

The plans for this course are for it to be offered fully online in the future.

Method
Managing Cyber Threats to Critical Infrastructure Protection was transitioned to a blended course by using myCourses discussions and the dropbox extensively.

During the preparation of the class, the calendar and e-mail features became useful tools to keep students informed. All course materials, except copyrighted textbooks, were made available through myCourses (including another text available online through the Government Printing Office).

The calendar and e-mail continued to be useful tools in broadcasting information to students, while individual communication was conducted via phone or e-mail.

Results
Discussions
Overall, the blended format worked very well for this course, especially the online discussions. The key was regular moderation of the discussion and control over the topic.

However, the discussion area was difficult to manage. It was also confusing at first. It was not readily obvious how to answer other posts.

Some students answered the previous individual-topic post while others made general posts to the discussion. This was confusing for the students as well as difficult for me to understand and moderate some of the threads.

To remedy this, the format should be made configurable by the instructor as to whether students can answer individual posts or simply post to the general discussion. Or, from an instructor level, coach the students on the use of the discussion feature. This takes valuable time away from the course material itself but may be a good interim resolution.

Difficulty coaching students with problems

Students that were having problems with participation and/or project work were extremely difficult to coach through cyberspace. The virtual aspect of the online component eliminates the ability of the instructor to read the body language and eye contact of the student. This is especially true with shy/quiet students who do not communicate well in the first place. They can acknowledge an e-mail or phone call without truly understanding it. It helps to have some physical interaction with students—a virtual rapport is totally different from an actual rapport.

Students who have poor social skills may flock to online programs. Once they graduate, they are no more emotionally prepared to enter the workforce than before they started. To remedy this, an instructor could require some non-virtual, face-to-face interaction with the student, either through a resident phase of an online program or a blended course format.

Clarity needed in project descriptions

Written descriptions of projects and assignments posted in myCourses were not always clear to the students. Some students read and understood the online assignment instructions without any problem, while others struggled with them. Often they would turn to each other for interpretation instead of the instructor for clarification. In the future, I could use examples of expected work products, posted online, to show format and content.

Conclusion

Overall the blended format worked very well. This was the first time this course was offered, so there was some tweaking to do on the course itself, but the format was suited to this course. I learned a lot from teaching it in the blended format which will only make it easier and more manageable the next time.

Postscript

Since my first experience with the blended format I have not been scheduled to teach it again until this fall. However, the original purpose of using the blended format was to transition the course to a fully online, asynchronous course format. The preparation for and conduct of the blended course helped to prepare me for the transition to the online course format.

"Overall, the blended course format worked very well for this course, especially the online discussions. The key was regular moderation of the discussion and control over the topic."

The value of having the course prepared in both formats is to accommodate different student demographics. I will always prefer to have the personal, one-to-one interaction with students whenever possible, but today's lifestyles do not always allow for that. Preparing the course in both formats allows the flexibility to accommodate either a remote student population or a local one.

Joseph Hennekey is an adjunct instructor of computer crime for the College of Liberal Arts and College of Applied Science and Technology.

Stephanie Ludi
Quantitative Methods of Delivering Usable Software
Software Engineering Department
College of Computing and Information Sciences
2004–2005 fall quarter

Background
I have taught various Software Engineering courses to primarily undergraduate software engineering students. I have utilized myCourses and other online resources to support instruction for several years. In myCourses, I have made lecture material (e.g. PowerPoint slides), readings, grades and project material available to students.

Objectives
During the fall 2004 quarter, I offered a seminar to address quantitative techniques that can be utilized in the delivery of usable software. With this seminar I wanted to promote various forms of discussion and reflection. This form of learning does not necessitate the traditional face-to-face classroom interaction. The Blended Pilot offered an opportunity to integrate new forms of interaction in my seminar.

Method
I offered Quantitative Methods of Delivering Usable Software to 16 undergraduate students in the blended format on campus.

The seminar was a four-credit course that counted towards the required two-course requirement in the design elective category. The course consisted of 16 undergraduate software engineering students—with one third-year and 15 fourth- and fifth-year students.

The objective of the blended course was to replace 25 percent of the face-to-face instruction with online activities conducted via myCourses, specifically the synchronous chat and asynchronous discussion features. The online activities consisted of student discussions, student-to-student critiques and virtual team meetings with the instructor.

Rather than a lecturer, I was a facilitator in the myCourses environment. I created areas where students could find project and assignment materials in addition to lecture slides. Online activities were primarily housed in the discussion forums, where questions and activities were posed for students to contribute or to discuss. In addition, special online office hours were conducted in a chat room in myCourses.

I was already proficient in myCourses, but the Online Learning department offered assistance in planning the logistics of the online activities. During the quarter I taught the course, the Blended Pilot luncheon with the other participants offered ideas and feedback to consider during this experience and for future blended courses.

> "Rather than a lecturer, I was a facilitator in the myCourses environment. The blended learning model showed students that learning can take place in various contexts."

The class met for two two-hour blocks per week. At the beginning of the quarter, five class meetings were allocated to online activities. However, two other class meetings were also conducted online due to my need to go out-of-town during the quarter. While the class meetings were called "online meetings," students could conduct the activities and discussions on their own time before the next face-to-face meeting. Only synchronous, virtual team meetings were conducted at specific times between the student teams and the instructor in order to discuss the status of the team project.

Each student was a member of two teams, their project team and their special topic team. The student chose their project team, but I randomly assigned students to four-person special-topic teams. The project team applied various techniques and even tested their software projects with actual users. The concept of the project team is similar to other teams that students have participated in previously. Project teams were also used for in-class activities. The special topic teams had an assigned (general) topic that related to usability. Each team needed to facilitate and moderate a running class discussion in the topic over the course of several weeks (Weeks 4 to 10). While each student was on a special topic team, they were also expected to participate in other topics as well.

The course grade had several components:

- Three exams—45 percent
- The team course project—30 percent
- In-class and online participation—10 percent
- Individual assignments—15 percent

Previous experience showed me that student participation in online discussions can be difficult to achieve. To motivate students to participate, I described my expectations for postings in special topics (e.g. at least two meaningful postings per week per person in their topic and one meaningful posting in another topic and I provided the definition of meaningful posting). These expectations, in addition to my intermittent participation in the discussions when needed, resulted in interesting discussion, sharing of resources and sharing of experiences.

Results

The blended learning model showed students that learning can take place in various contexts. Students procrastinated less on project assignments. While student postings to online discussions tended to be during the weekend, the quality of the postings was high. I learned as much from them as did the other students in the class—as the students have had interesting co-op experiences that they could draw from. A significantly larger percentage of students actively participated online than before, either online or in class.

People may assume that students and faculty in computing disciplines utilize technology effectively for instruction. Beyond the computing concepts, the logistics and new applications of technology are not always found in these courses. Students are computer literate, but using technology to support their learning and reflection is still new to them. I would recommend blended learning to other instructors, particularly for upper-division or graduate courses. The Online Learning department offers support for interested instructors, which is extremely helpful throughout the course offering.

Modifications

For those interested in pursuing the utilization of the blended learning format in a course, I suggest the following items that were successful for me:

- Clearly define the expectations for online student participation
- Encourage student sharing of resources
- Provide early feedback to students regarding online participation
- Keep class sizes small or be able to divide the class into subsets in order to foster community
- Deliberately connect material from online discussions in the face-to-face meetings to promote the integration of material

- Spend sufficient time before the course starts to plan the class schedule and topic distribution

- Be flexible and open to new ideas

While not a recipe for success, these points offer a starting point for a faculty member who is starting out or considering the blended learning format. Finding your own community with others, including Online Learning staff, will be worth your effort.

Stephanie Ludi is an assistant professor in the software engineering department of the B. Thomas Golisano College of Computing and Information Sciences.

Tom Reichlmayr
Software Engineering I
Software Engineering Department
Computing and Information Sciences
2004–2005 fall quarter

Objectives

Software Engineering I is an introductory software engineering course required by all Software Engineering, Computer Science and Computer Engineering majors. The course has a heavy project flavor with teams of students participating in a quarter-long software development effort. With so much focus on the project, a primary objective of blending this course was to make the in-class time spent by students in their project teams more effective.

As students were also responsible for meeting in teams outside of scheduled class time, another objective was to provide tools and methods for teams to collaborate more effectively using online resources. Today's commercial software development environment is growing more and more reliant on the ability of geographically distributed teams of engineers to work together in similar "virtual development labs" on common projects and products.

Method

Prior to blending this class, it had been redesigned over the past two years and achieved a significant online presence. The course is delivered in studio lab format with three hours of traditional lecture and two hours of lab per week being replaced with two two-hour sessions of combined lecture and lab sessions. Students are divided into teams of five developers the first week and remain together throughout the quarter. All course and project material is available online using the myCourses course management system.

The move to the studio lab format had already decreased the amount of in-class face time by one hour per week. This move was supported by moving a significant amount of traditional lecture time into online resources in the form of self-study and online discussion activities. The blended addition for this quarter focused on the team project aspect of the course.

During the project, instructors take the role of surrogates for the customer. Teams must interact with the customer to elicit requirements for the product. In a typical session, this would require the instructor using class project time to meet with each team. The approach in the blended course was to establish scheduled synchronous online chats with the "customer." This encouraged teams to be more focused and prepared when meeting with the customer, as well as helping the instructor manage the interactions with four and sometimes eight different project teams. The time normally consumed by customer-elicitation activity was now available for other project development activities and opportunity for additional instructor interaction on other facets of the project.

"The comment that best captured the blending learning experience was, 'I liked that the course was a combination of self-learning / hands-on activities, rather than a course just being taught to you by an instructor.'"

The blended activities for the course also included moving two quizzes and a graded class activity from an in-class format to online activities using the quizzing and discussion features of myCourses.

Results

As our students are more technically inclined, they did not have the technology issues sometimes encountered by other courses using online tools and techniques. There was, however, the need to make students aware of the differences in using online communications tools in a professional environment, as opposed to their more informal interactions. In this regard, the quality of the chat sessions improved throughout the quarter as the teams acclimated themselves to the professional tone of the conversations.

It was also evident that teams had taken time prior to the chat to prepare a strategy for the elicitation session. Teams were made aware to make good use of limited time when chatting with the customer. The lesson being that typical customers are rarely as available as your instructor is when questions arise.

Each team participated in two to three customer chat sessions throughout the quarter. An interesting observation was that, for the first chat, some teams physically met in the lab and huddled around one terminal while the chat was taking place. During future chats, teams found it more convenient to use the power of virtual meetings to participate from remote locations. The chats were also quite valuable to the instructor in being able use the logs to document conversations with student teams and maintaining consistency in the responses. Prior sessions were often a collection of undocumented, informal responses as questions were posed by the project teams in an ad-hoc manner. It also allows the opportunity to vary the requirements between project teams.

We are always looking for innovations to support the studio format for this and other software engineering courses. The experiences gained through the Blended Pilot will be applied to the continuing improvement of our program.

Postscript

Since my initial experience with our introductory software engineering course, I have had several opportunities to bring blended learning into the classroom.

One particular experience that stands out is an upper division seminar class on Agile Software Development. This particular approach to software development advocates a highly collaborative environment with developers working in small teams using a methodology known as extreme programming. My plan for the seminar was to equally split class time in our studio lab between this team-based development activity and exploring topics and trends in agile software development. As the course began to quickly fill during registration, it became apparent that the assigned studio lab would not be able to accommodate the space required for the team projects. We ended up adopting a blended approach (later dubbed as "Extreme Blended") which split the class in two, with half the students using the lab during one meeting time each week for the team project and then using online resources (chat, discussion forums) for lecture and research activities. It was a unique situation for most of the students (and their instructor) and all responded enthusiastically.

The end of course survey comment that best captured the blending learning experience was, "I liked that the course was a combination of self-learning / hands-on activities, rather than a course just being taught to you by an instructor."

Tom Reichlmayr is an associate professor in the software engineering department in the B. Thomas Golisano College of Computing and Information Sciences.

Elizabeth Lawley
Web Design and Implementation
Information Technology Department
College of Computing and Information Sciences
2004-2005 winter quarter

Background

I had been teaching Web Design and Implementation for several years, always in a studio model—two hours, twice a week, with a mix of lecture and hands-on exercises. However, this model often resulted in students who completed work quickly waiting for others to finish their work, or for those who didn't finish quickly enough to get lost when I moved on to the next portion of the lecture.

Method

For the blended learning version of the class, I chose to consolidate the lecture material on the first class meeting of the week and use the second class meeting as an optional studio time for students to work on exercises with me or their peers. This meant I had to provide the in-class exercises online and have a way to evaluate them online as well, since some students would choose not to attend the studio sessions.

Instead of myCourses, I used the MovableType weblog-based courseware to make the exercises, readings and materials available to students and required each of them to create their own MovableType weblog to use as a portfolio site. Their exercises had to be written up and posted to their weblogs and linked back to the entry on the class site. This allowed me to see their work, but also allowed them to see each other's work and learn from it.

Using MovableType in a web design class provides a dual value, because it gives them an environment in which they can implement many of the class topics—CSS, Javascript, CGI scripts, etc.—in a way that also allows them to talk about those topics. Not all students liked the weblogs, but many of them liked them enough to start their own private weblogs.

I made the Wednesday studio session entirely voluntary, with the exception of the day we did a group-project exercise and the day they took their practical exam. I expected that on most days, no more than 10-15 of the 37 students in the class would attend—but I was surprised (and pleased) to find that at least two-thirds, often more, of the students attended on a regular basis. Because it was an open work time, they could work at their own pace on the things they were interested in and didn't have to compare their pace to other students' or try to keep up with the lecture at the same time. Many of them also used the time for group meetings, which are often very difficult for students with busy work schedules to manage. I believe this contributed to the fact that the quality of the group projects for this class was significantly higher than in most of my other web design classes.

Conclusion

Overall, I thought this was a very effective way to teach the class, because it gave me regular in-person time with the students—something I find important in teaching—as well as providing the students with greater flexibility in how they approached the material.

Elizabeth Lawley is an associate professor in the information technology department in B. Thomas Golisano College of Computing and Information Sciences.

Deaf Education

Christine Monikowski
Introduction to the Field of Interpreting &
Discourse Analysis for Interpreters
Department of ASL and Interpreting Education
National Technical Institute for the Deaf
2005-2006 fall and winter quarters

Objectives

I wanted to support a goal that appears in the syllabus for the Introduction to the Field of Interpreting course: *Develop reading, writing, speaking, analytical thinking and problem solving skills related to the role and function of an interpreter.*

I also wanted to support an implicit objective in the Discourse Analysis for Interpreters course that I introduce on the first day: *Provide students with the opportunity to consider their answers before they participate in classroom activities.*

Spontaneous classroom discussions and activities target a variety of student learning styles, but these activities are often "performance" rather than substance. I've offered a number of online courses for a variety of institutions around the country and I believe that writing is important for interpreting students; it gives them time to reflect on their own thoughts and decisions:

> "Why does writing improve thinking? Skill in thinking is like musical and athletic skills. It takes practice to improve—particularly practice that enables one to see what works and what doesn't. Much of our thinking remains in our minds, where it is not exposed to review. The very process of putting thoughts to paper forces clarification; seeing them on paper (or on the computer screen) facilitates our own evaluation; and receiving comments from peers or teachers provides further help. Note that most of these educational gains do not require that writing be graded. Writing is to facilitate learning and thinking. Thinking in turn results in class discussions that are animated and thoughtful." —McKeachie, W.J. 2002. *Teaching Tips*. Boston: Houghton Mifflin (p. 170-171)

Method

In Introduction to the Field of Interpreting, 10 postings were required for the fall quarter class. Postings were pass/fail:

- PASS = Excellent; work is complete and content shows analysis; clearly exceeds minimum requirements; spelling and grammar are accurate

- FAIL = Unsatisfactory; work is complete but shows little analysis; deficiencies in quality; spelling and grammar are problematic

"Thoughtful reflection about professional topics is something that I always want my students to appreciate. Our field is filled with interpreters who can do the work, but who cannot discuss the work that they do."

Every student received in-depth feedback on their first two postings; I made it very clear whether these were pass/fail. There were numerous questions and answers among all of us but, by the third posting, I felt confident that they understood the quality of work that I expected. Although there were several lapses during the quarter, on the whole, the quality of their work was very good and we were all able to attend to the content, rather than "how many sentences do I need to post," etc.

Discourse Analysis for Interpreters also required 10 postings. Because most of the students (29 out of 31) in the second course had been in the first course, I expected more from them on their postings. There was no "training time" where they had to learn how to post, where to post, how much to post, etc. We hit the ground running and the quality of their work was outstanding.

Results

Thoughtful reflection about professional topics is something that I always want my students to appreciate. Our field is filled with interpreters who can do the work, but who cannot discuss the work that they do! I want more for my students and I believe that thoughtful reflection gives them the opportunity to consider their peers' perspectives and also to develop an understanding of their own perspectives.

As an offshoot of the fall quarter course, five students wanted to explore the question from an assigned article: What do interpreters think about a classic theoretical discussion in the profession? Over the winter and spring quarters, students developed and piloted questions. With some advice from RIT's Online Learning department, they created an online survey and learned about qualitative research and the Institute Review Board along the way. Fifty-eight interpreters from NTID/RIT's Department of Access Services and Monroe County's BOCES #1 responded. Students were excited about the positive comments they got from working interpreters who recognize the need for such innovative research. I'm thrilled that such an exciting experience resulted from my required postings!

I firmly believe that these students would not have gotten involved in this project if we had not had our online discussions; in fact, I doubt that they would have seen the possibility of such a project. Over the years, there have been numerous times when I tried to encourage students to do an independent project, a survey, etc.; I have a file drawer filled with beginnings. The comfort these five students have with online work is, I believe, a major factor in the progress they are making.

Postscript

In the three years since I participated in RIT's Blended Learning Pilot, there have been two major activities that resulted from that time.

First, the research project that students began culminated in a Clipboard survey of working interpreters (N = 75) and several presentations of that data. One was for the NTID Advisory Group, in April 2007, who was duly impressed with this undergraduate project. Another was for a May 2007 presentation at the NY state convention which was very well-received by working interpreters.

Secondly, I have added an online component to all of my content courses. I still require quite a bit of online discussions for Introduction to the Field of Interpreting, which happens during the students' first quarter in our program. But our Practical and Ethical Considerations course is offered their fifth quarter so my expectations of quality participation are higher. When I first began my involvement with blended learning, I had said that I wanted students to have time to consider their comments and the online component allowed for that. In the Ethics course, reflection is even more important because the work is more challenging. Students spend time discussing dilemmas, possible resolutions, add input from working interpreters and include perspectives from deaf consumers.

The McKeachie quote I originally cited which addresses the importance of writing and its connection to thinking, is still important and one of the foundations of my teaching.

Christine Monikowski is an associate professor in the department of ASL and interpreting education at the National Technical Institute for the Deaf.

Paula Doane
Electrical/Mechanical Design CAD
Industrial Science and Technologies Department
National Technical Institute for the Deaf
2004–2005 spring quarter

Objective

In blending this course, one of the objectives was to develop writing skills in a technical course tailored to deaf and hard-of-hearing students. Since most of the course was to be done online—a written environment—students were required to write under these conditions more often. Good writing skills enable students to better communicate with engineers on the job after graduation. Another objective of blending the course was to increase interaction between students, as reducing the face-to-face time would represent an increase in written communication among students.

Method

I divided the course roughly in half into in-class time and online interaction (synchronous chat and asynchronous discussion). We spent the first few weeks in a traditional face-to-face setting, meeting three times a week. I also developed myCourses exercises to establish some knowledge with the technology and methods. From the third week on, we met twice a week in the classroom and had an online activity in place of the other day of class.

I was always available in chat sessions online on the days the class would have met. The purpose of the chat sessions was mainly to maintain interaction with students and to answer questions about assignments. In general, about 50 to 60 percent of the students were in the general chat sessions.

Online activities always involved the course project. Students read a topic related to the project and posted their response in an online discussion forum. Students then responded to their classmates and finally wrote a summary of the online discussion, which they handed in at the following classroom meeting.

I monitored the online discussions. The team leader or I set up a meeting once a week during class time to follow up on the project and its deadlines. We used the discussion forum to set up the meetings and prepare to meet in the classroom. The discussion was also used to keep things moving to finish on deadline and make sure the team split up project tasks—such as assembly, electrical drawings, mechanical drawings, etc.—and deadlines. To get credit, students had to log their discussion of the topic and come to an agreement on who was doing what.

Results

Students responded really well to this technique of instruction. Since I taught this same course with the same materials the previous year, I had a good opportunity for comparison. What I wanted to accomplish was to encourage students to use discussion and writing skills to communicate so that they feel more confident and comfortable in the workforce.

In these online discussions, I did not grade for grammar. The purpose of this exercise was for effective communication and engagement with ideas. Students were encouraged to exchange ideas freely without being wrong or insulted. In their online activities, students were free to use language without correction.

In comparison with the traditional course format, in a face-to-face setting students did not discuss as much and kept to themselves more rather than sharing with each other. Final grades in the blended course, as compared with my traditional course, were generally higher, with an average of A and B online compared with average grades of B and C.

Finally, in the blended course, students wrote more, were more interactive with their classmates and thus received higher grades overall. I am very impressed with how well the students did in the course.

Postscript

I have used blended learning since teaching this course. My experience has shown that it's a great method of teaching and very helpful for students to keep communication open. When I teach another course at RIT, I will continue to use a blended format for lab/class courses. It helps teams work together very well. Every year I learn more and myCourses becomes more user-friendly with easy-to-use tools. It also helps my teaching by allowing me to keep all resources together to use in future courses.

Paula Doane is a senior engineer in mechanical design for GENTEX Corp. in Simpson, Penn.

Vincent Samar

Teaching Deaf Learners with Secondary Disorders
Department of Research and Teacher Education
National Technical Institute for the Deaf
2004–2005 spring quarter

Background

This course focuses on providing students with a basic understanding of the nature and needs of deaf learners with secondary disabilities, including (1) learning disability, (2) attention deficit hyperactivity disorder, (3) developmental disability, (4) emotional or behavioral disorder, and (5) visual impairment.

The purpose of this course is to prepare students to see deaf learners with secondary disabilities from multiple perspectives, including the perspectives of parent, teacher, school psychologist, researcher, clinician and therapist. To accomplish this, the course features parents and deafness professionals as weekly presenters who share their personal and professional experiences of dealing with children who are deaf or hard-of-hearing and have secondary disabilities.

Students are responsible for writing and posting online weekly papers that incorporate information from assigned reading materials and from information they find themselves online. Students interact online in myCourses regarding their weekly papers and also write a final paper either individually or in small groups.

Objectives

Traditionally, this course has been taught as a four-hour face-to-face classroom session once a week in the evening. Typically, one hour of that time would be used for classroom discussion. One of the objectives of blending this course was to allow the discussion component to occur online, asynchronously, over an extended period of several days, rather than on the heels of an already exhausting three hours of focused presentations. Accordingly, in-class time was reduced to three hours and online postings and interactive discussion activities were required during the week following the in-class presentations.

A second objective of blending this course was to provide deaf, hard-of-hearing and hearing students with an effective online option for spontaneously communicating with their peers throughout the quarter regarding their ideas and experiences as student teachers.

A third objective of blending this course was to provide students the opportunity to find and share electronic resources online.

Method

During each three-hour weekly class, students listened to one or two lengthy presentations or they observed a panel discussion. A note taker took and later distributed notes electronically to the class.

Outside of class, students wrote a two-page summary of the presentations, based on class notes and their own teaching experiences, and integrated information from assigned weekly readings. They also were responsible for finding an article or authoritative website related to the weekly topic and including a link to the site in their summary. They posted their summaries on myCourses discussion boards by the third day after the weekly class.

Over the next three days, each student read all of the posted summaries and then selected one summary and posted a response to it for other students to read. I graded the weekly papers and responded to each student online.

In addition, students were encouraged to post discussion topics as separate threads on the myCourses discussion board that were inspired by their own concerns or by something that had come up during class.

Results

The approach of using asynchronous online discussion via weekly papers provided students with the opportunity and time to reflect thoughtfully on the presentation content and to integrate what they learned in class with the weekly readings. The overall result was a more refreshed, informed and protracted interaction among students that occurred somewhat spontaneously throughout the week.

Instead of attending a series of single weekly class discussions throughout the quarter and then disengaging from the topic between classes, students now experienced the ever-present option of engaging themselves in a relevant intellectual and professional community activity throughout the entire quarter. Although students were only required to post twice during the week (i.e., a summary and a response to another student's summary) they nevertheless tended to continue the discussion initiated by each other's responses throughout the week.

The online component offered on-demand participatory access for all students, which, in my opinion, reinforced the learning process by providing augmented exposure to concepts and new reading materials during the lull between weekly classes.

Conducting discussions online provided a text-based option that allowed the entire class to interact with each other directly between classes throughout the quarter. Deaf, hard-of-hearing and hearing students who have various levels of proficiency in sign language and in spoken and written communication typically attend this class. Both face-to-face and online interactions present some communication barriers for different students. Therefore, it is important to have options for communicating with peers that include efficient electronic sharing of text as well as the more traditional face-to-face interaction during class using sign and speech.

> *"Themes that inspired both mutual agreement and spirited debate arose. The online medium permitted the entire class to play out these themes between class sessions as a cohesive participatory community."*

Future online discussion software should be developed that facilitates the use of video postings and video responses as organized threads. This functionality would further extend the communication options available to students for online asynchronous discussions by allowing the use of sign language and would help to bridge the language and culture gap between deaf and hearing students in the same class.

Requiring each student to share online resources magnified the cache of readings and informational materials available in the course. One highly satisfying consequence of this requirement was that some students uncovered valuable parent and teacher guides to various secondary disabilities. All of the students in this class were delighted to have such materials to use in their own teaching careers in the near future.

In addition to their assignment-related interactions, students spontaneously posted interesting discussion topics. Some topics were related to teaching techniques and issues. Others were related to more sensitive cultural and language issues that concern the deaf community and its hearing allies. Themes that inspired both mutual agreement and spirited debate arose over the course of the quarter, and the online medium permitted the entire class to play out these themes between class sessions as a cohesive participatory community.

Modifications

I expect to expand my use of online technology with future classes. One particularly interesting idea that I expect to implement is to have experts from around the country present to the class via video or web conferencing. A second innovation that I expect to implement is to give all presenters access to the myCourses discussion boards so that they can interact asynchronously with the class during the week after their presentation.

Vincent Samar is an associate professor in the research and teacher education department in the National Technical Institute for the Deaf.

James Mallory
Programming II in Visual Basic
Applied Computer Technology Department
National Technical Institute for the Deaf
2004–2005 winter quarter

Background

Programming II in Visual Basic is a second course in a two-course programming sequence; most of the students are deaf or hard-of-hearing. Students already have been exposed to introductory programming concepts and are learning more advanced data structures and objects in this blended class. I was concerned about experimenting with blended learning in the first programming course in the sequence, as this material tended to be overwhelming for our Associate degree-level students and the students themselves were not always mature, motivated learners.

This three-credit course normally meets on Monday, Wednesday and Friday. In my blended version of the course, the Monday and Wednesday classes were held as usual, and the Friday classes were substituted with synchronous, web conferencing sessions, which were held on four Fridays.

Objectives

The objective of this blended course was to combine two traditional programming classes and empower students to become more independent learners in the computer programming area.

Methods

Static materials were posted not in myCourses, but on my own course website; these included:

- Downloadable programming examples

- Homework assignments with both English explanations and executable demonstration files

- RealPlayer streamed multimedia examples using four video streams including voice, captioning, screen capture sequences and sign language explanations by the instructor

- Media Player streamed multimedia examples using JavaScript explanations and screen sequence explanations

Except for web broadcasting, dynamic activities were implemented through myCourses. These activities included posting students' executable files of programs that they created and asynchronous discussions with the instructor and between students.

Instead of the myCourses chat tool, I used a non-RIT proprietary web conferencing tool (which I paid for on my own) that allowed me to use the synchronous chat with students and, at the same time, to post sections of program code and use white board drawing tools to explain and emphasize different aspects of each program. The application sharing feature of the program was a great tool for tutoring students remotely. I also used a webcam just to let students see me and my facial expressions for communication; the webcam was not adequate for sign language use. On a few of the web conferences, I used video phones which incorporate compression technology and are adequate for remote sign language use.

Results

Getting students to participate online asynchronously was a struggle in the beginning, even though participation was six percent of the overall grade for the course. To improve the response, I had students post their weekly programming assignment executable file on myCourses and comment and vote on each other's programs. The top two students who received the most votes on each assignment received an additional 10 percent extra credit for that particular programming assignment. This seemed to work well. Not only did students participate more, but the quality of their assignments also improved. They seemed to take pride in creating and sharing their programs and they also were competing with each other to earn the extra credit, which some of them desperately needed.

The blended classroom seemed to work well for the sharper and mid-range student. The sharp students enjoyed the flexibility of working on their own time and being able to work independently. The blended class was great for the mid-range student who was required to learn more independently and work with other students to solve programming problems and questions. For the slower students, however, blended did not seem to be a good fit. Even if the programs, code, examples, executables and multimedia were posted online and online discussions were used, both synchronous and asynchronous, these students would still come to my office to ask the same questions, even if they were already explained on the website or through other means. From an instructor's perspective, this is not necessarily a bad thing. My time was spent with students who really needed my experience with teaching and tutoring, as opposed to delivering one traditional lecture each week to students who would be better off learning more independently.

Combining two separate sections of the class into one online conference seemed to work well. Synergism was created from the joint efforts of more students from two separate smaller classes interacting in the same electronic conference and in the same web broadcast. The online interactive portion of the blended class allowed some female and other shy students who were normally passive in class to participate more readily.

Overall, the amount and quality of interactions among deaf and hard-of-hearing students and between these same students and me, a hearing instructor, seemed to be higher than in a traditional classroom once extra credit, interactive activities were developed, which can really help boost their grade. As predicted, if an online activity was not tied to their final grade, then most students did not participate.

> "The amount and quality of interactions among deaf and hard-of-hearing students and between the students and me, seemed to be higher than in a traditional classroom."

James Mallory is a professor in the information and computing studies department at the National Technical Institute for the Deaf.

Pamela Conley
Written Communication II
Department of Liberal Studies
National Technical Institute for the Deaf
2006-2007 fall quarter

Background

Written Communication II assists deaf and hard-of-hearing students in developing the necessary writing and reading skills to successfully complete Writing Seminar, a writing course required for graduation. In Written Communications II, students are required to demonstrate the ability to do research by electronic means to write successful essays. Students are also expected to:

- Demonstrate the ability to use certain strategies to read basic college-level texts—by employing strategies of annotating, outlining and summarizing texts

- Recognize purpose, audience and tone in assigned reading selection

- Engage in activities pertaining to the process of writing such as pre-drafting, drafting, revising, editing, proofreading and preparing the final draft

One's success as a reader and writer depends on one's ability to do all kinds of writing. Electronic messages are one type of writing students can expect to prepare—for upper-level courses at NTID/RIT as well as on the job after they graduate. Even though it is considered to be routine, writing an electronic message still demands a great deal of thought and time. This strongly reinforces one of the objectives of the course—serious consideration of one's audience's needs and expectations and formats for effective written communication.

Objectives

The goal of blending the course was to incorporate technology to address student learning needs specific to Written Communication II. Introducing the online discussion board feature in myCourses was intended to generate dialogue outside of class. It was also intended to serve as a springboard for further in-class discussion about a wide range of topics about academic writing and relevant topics for in-class and out-of-class essays.

Students were required to engage in weekly online discussions, which consisted of prompt questions that were based on the assigned chapters of a required text called *They Say, I Say*. I prepared questions, asking students to paraphrase or summarize the content of each chapter and to offer comments, either evaluative or judgmental in nature.

Method

On the first day of class, I delivered a brief lecture on how to constructively use the online discussion forums. Additional information about the use of the discussion board was available in the course syllabus.

> "Students using the discussion forum demonstrated increased participation in activities within the classroom. Rates of appropriate responses to class discussions were much higher than those without the benefit of the online discussion forum."

Eight postings were required for the fall quarter class. The most frequently asked question by students about the first three postings was in reference to formatting issues. However, this problem was gradually resolved over time as I repeatedly explained my expectations in class. Some students continued to have problems with the discussion board after my intervention, so I called them to my office where I reviewed the discussion forum step-by-step.

Students thought they had put their responses appropriately. Their versions tended to be brief and superficial. I provided feedback on the early postings in the discussions, but decided to stop posting my comments publicly. Some students got discouraged knowing that other students read my constructive comments specifically written for them. Instead, I offered sometimes general and sometimes in-depth feedback on the quality of postings at the beginning of each class to ensure anonymity and confidentiality of every respondent.

Results

The introduction of the discussion forum as one required component of writing for the course was challenging. Students had to familiarize themselves in using the technology. They became fully comfortable in using the board after the third week of the quarter. I also felt I was partially accountable for lack of structure as it relates to using the discussion forum, which compounded the early difficulties students experienced in using the technology.

Students using the discussion forum outside of the classroom demonstrated increased participation in activities within the classroom. Rates of appropriate responses to class discussions were much higher than those without the benefit of the online discussion forum.

As the course progressed, using the discussion forum significantly facilitated conversations between students and me as their instructor, reducing significant amounts of time I traditionally spend in class to clarify assignments and address maintenance issues.

While the discussion forum is a good way of encouraging active student participation, it can lead to inactive participation for some students, especially the ones lacking strong reading and writing skills and abilities. Some students read their peers' already submitted responses before developing their own responses. This discouraged the struggling students from strengthening their reading and writing skills. Also, using the discussion forum, which was intended to elicit meaningful student participation, often led to students being interested in competing with their peers rather than mastering the material.

All in all, I was initially disappointed by the quality of student work in the early postings. However, I had to remind myself that students and I did not have the benefit of this technology prior to being involved in this project. With added practice and experience, I believe that my proficiency in using the discussion board in eliciting appropriate student responses will improve.

Postscript

Although I'm not presently teaching any blended courses, they make it much easier for me and my students to work together. A blended course is an academic model that emulates a professional model of how employees and employers typically interact in today's workplace. My students, who are mostly deaf or hard-of-hearing, benefit from blended courses tremendously, as they utilize written English much more than they do in traditional courses.

In blended courses, students actually engage in activities of reading and following instructions and writing frequently, which reinforce the ultimate goal of the writing courses I teach—have students read critically as well as demonstrate successful written communications.

As an instructor who is not so tech-savvy, I find the blended design greatly reduces my initial preparation time for courses I teach again and again. It also allows me to have the time to rework some of my materials to keep the overall course content current and exciting. Additionally, I have become much comfortable in seeking technical support if I am unable to resolve technical issues on my own. All in all, I believe blended courses enable students and me to acquire and maintain a set of skills needed to make important contributions in our future communities.

Pamela Conley is an associate professor in the liberal studies department at the National Technical Institute for the Deaf.

Humanities

Kristine Fredrick
Academic English
English Language Center
Division of Student Affairs
2007-2008 fall quarter

Background

I had taught either Academic English 1 or 2 in the evening for four quarters prior to my first blended course experience. The course uses a textbook and video for simulating the college classroom environment to increase English language learners' comprehension and fluency in their academic courses. Each time I have taught the course, I supplement and replace different textbook activities with actual classroom visits and experiences and use more engaging media to exercise comprehension and fluency. The rapid increase in available technology makes it important to engage students in comprehension and fluency with the technology used in college classrooms. Thus, I requested that Academic English 1 for the fall 2007 quarter be listed as a blended course and that I be allowed to designate some of the seat time as outside-of-class online time.

Objective

The syllabus stated the following objectives:

Students in this course will practice listening and speaking skills necessary for use in the American college classroom. We will focus on note-taking, computer and study strategies, questioning skills, discussion and response in the classroom, written standards, idiomatic expressions and building reading comprehension. We will also focus on expanding our vocabulary.

This is a blended course which means you will be expected to use the Internet to participate in online class and group meetings, to read and research on line, and to submit online drafts of written work.

The objective of the course continues to focus on comprehension and fluency but now includes more media fluency and more interactive technology with which students must be fluent to succeed in university courses.

Method

I divided each class meeting into four major sections: readings, media, collaboration, and grammar and writing.

The reading section focuses on comprehension and vocabulary building. We review texts and media assigned for homework and introduce some new materials on similar topics. We complete text, team or discussion activities to assess comprehension, as well as to generate analysis, synthesis and interpretation of the materials.

"Teaching a blended course allowed me to be more creative in distributing materials, assigning tasks and using technology."

The media section of the lesson focuses the class on listening comprehension. I provide a film or audio feature to watch or listen to and then have students respond with vocabulary collection, idiom usage and a discussion of the content as well as some student journal writing to synthesize the new words or information. These responses were posted online. Thus they had an online record of journal entries or "posts."

The collaboration section was a new section that I included in the blended format to encourage students to work together outside of class. They had to meet outside of class or communicate online to develop activities and study vocabulary. Next time, I will have them do a different collaborative project using vocabulary. I think I will have each team design a slide show to teach vocabulary rather than designing vocabulary games. That was hard for some students to engage in.

The collaboration that is usual in the course is for students to peer edit each other's papers. That worked well online because I could see the threads of comments and give credit for reading and posting suggestions. It also took that activity out of the classroom and left more time in class for different kinds of discussion. I will continue to do that in all my courses.

Results

Two added benefits of this course came after meeting my participants. The students always come from many programs and many backgrounds. This course included one American HEOP student, an international NTID student who is deaf, and three au pairs from Germany and Vietnam in addition to our ELC students from Asia and the Middle East. The blended course allowed me to make a wide variety of media available to my students. It allowed me to narrow their research sources and to scaffold the instruction for gathering, note taking, drafting, writing and citing sources in the research process. At every step I was able to be sure students were paraphrasing and citing sources properly.

My students largely preferred the use of digital submissions and online meetings for discussion. My deaf student and au pairs found this extremely helpful, but for different reasons. The au pairs had a hard time getting out to RIT at night on time for class and staying so late due to their early mornings and long work schedule. So they appreciated a later meeting time coupled with an online discussion on an alternative night or an early dismissal coupled with an online discussion group on a different night. The 20-minute difference, either early or later, helped their attitude toward attending on other nights. The NTID student preferred the online sessions because he was able to follow the discussion. In our class meeting, interpreters were not always available and I am not a fast or proficient user of ASL.

One or two students reported that reducing class meeting time was not effective and that they preferred meeting in person rather than online. One student had problems submitting papers in the drop box because she did not have a compatible word processor application. There seems always to be one international student in the class who has an incompatible program, printer or interface of some kind that slows down the possibility of turning work in on time.

Conclusion

Using an online discussion tool during our actual class meetings might imitate the use of C-print in the absence of an interpreter. In future courses, I will try to get some of the videos uploaded to our site so they are available for viewing online rather than during course time. To do that, I need to have the video captioned, since it is not. It is a VHS tape, so it also needs to be digitized and loaded online for the course. I will begin this process in May or June, to hopefully be ready by next fall.

Postscript

I continue to use the myCourses platform to provide instruction, literature and discussion space for my students. I have not taught the blended course again since fall quarter, but I will teach it next fall and will offer the blended format again if it is approved by our program director. During the summer quarter, I teach in the English Language Center's Intensive English Program, where the students are in language programming all day, all week long. The situation is different in the fall and summer quarters. In the fall Academic English course, many of the students are enrolled in one or more courses from their degree program. They may not be taking any other English Language Center courses. So, the blended learning format allows them more access to language support in the fall when they are not in language classes every day.

Although none of the summer courses are blended courses, the online platform could still be used to supplement and increase the level of immersion that the Summer Intensive English program provides.

Teaching a blended course allowed me to be more creative in distributing materials, assigning tasks and using technology. I use online tools and platforms as a student in graduate programs, and as part of my usual communication with friends and family. I think it is important that we include threaded discussion, message boards, drop boxes and streaming or podcasting as part of the usual coursework for students preparing to be part of the North American university classroom. International students who have not had exposure to these tools need their language programs to introduce them—and to introduce the grammar, diction and protocol that go along with online learning—in order for students to differentiate online social communication from online academics. I learned that students, whether nationals or internationals, might not make linguistic distinctions between online learning, professional networking and social networking online. Teaching with a focus on different formats reveals to the students that they must vary their diction based on the format and context.

This blended course and the reflection on the process of using online learning has trained me to continuously consider digital media, linking resources, posting, discussions and video as a usual part of my lesson and curriculum design

> *"The reflection on the process of using blended learning has trained me to continuously consider digital media, linking resources, posting, discussions and video as a usual part of my lesson and curriculum design."*

Kristine Frederick is an adjunct instructor in the English Language Center in the Student Affairs Division.

Thomas Stone
Arts of Expression
Department of English
College of Liberal Arts
2005-2006 spring quarter

Objectives

Having taught online learning courses for several years, I was excited about the opportunity to combine the best of what online communication offers with the immediacy of a classroom experience. More specifically, I hoped to use the myCourses courseware management system to help students engage the readings in a more sustained and mature fashion.

Online tools foster student interaction in a way that is particularly advantageous to a course that emphasizes writing skills. My hope was that moving some discussion online would not only instill a certain rigor in the students' discourse but, since their interaction would be through messages posted to the class-wide discussion area, they would get valuable experience in formulating their thoughts in writing as well.

Method

I divided the classroom time in half. The class was taught on Monday and Wednesday. We began the week like a traditional classroom section on Monday, but we didn't meet on Wednesdays—using that time to complete whatever assignments I had posted online.

When I first began designing a blended course, I was stuck in the mindset that the online portion of the class was somehow ancillary, serving as a sort of footnote, confirming or clarifying what had already been discussed in class. I then realized that I should draw on the strengths of the online classes I had already been teaching.

So, instead, I highlighted the online interface—introducing students to the course material in that venue and having them respond in cyberspace before we ever sat in a room together.

Our classroom time could then be more productive and used much more efficiently. By the time we met, students had already read, considered and responded to the weekly readings.

To do that, I set up a series of weekly online discussion topics. For each week, I posted my instructions with quick links to the required reading. I came to rely fairly heavily on these instructions, for they contained not only whatever reading and discussion questions I wished to use, but they were also a good opportunity for me to add some comments of my own, contextualizing the readings, explaining difficult passages, bringing up the larger course themes, etc. I would generally get these materials posted a week ahead of time, so that by the time we came into the classroom, the students already had a considerable length of time to digest the reading material and share their thoughts with one another.

> *'I sometimes brought my computer into class and, using a portable projector, put the whole discussion thread on the screen. They then had all their work before them and I could flag individual messages to display.'*

Also, instead of having to waste time by, say, breaking them into small groups (answering questions on the reading or formulating a response), I could jump right in where their discussion left off and we could use our classroom time to build on, and go beyond, the conversation they had already started online.

In fact, I sometimes brought my computer into class and, using a portable projector, put the whole discussion thread on the screen. They then had all their work before them and I could flag individual messages to display, referring to the author sitting there in front of me. Sometimes I would not bring in the projector and computer, for I would instead print up all the messages in the weekly topic. This also worked well, for I had all of their messages in my hand and could refer quite specifically to what people had said in their posts.

This epitomizes what is so promising about the blended learning format. For, unlike a true distance learning course, I can communicate with the student about her post in a direct and visceral way that also draws in all the others, and we can then build on these ideas. And, unlike a traditional classroom section, I already have some sort of response from the student before I even walk into the classroom.

This process also helped to alert me to any areas of concern which I could then address in class (was something frequently misunderstood, for instance, or perhaps an exciting new direction was introduced in a post).

I also used myCourses as a mechanism to exchange peer responses on their final writing projects and, in addition to this, I used the dropbox for their last two writing assignments.

Results

Generally speaking, I was very impressed with the way things turned out. I felt that students had a better grasp of the issues we were exploring, and had mastered the reading material more fully than what I would generally expect from a classroom section. This evaluation, of course, remains somewhat impressionistic, but it is based on three different forms of evaluation: a final exam, essays written about the reading material and the general tenor of the class discussions.

The first four or five weeks in particular were quite stunning in their contrast to a typical classroom section. This 300-level class was eager and well informed. I was impressed not only with their grasp of the subject matter, but also with their nuanced, considered approach to these texts. The students appreciated the extra time at their disposal on the days we did not meet and, perhaps because this gave them greater control over how they managed their own time, nobody complained about the extra work the blended learning format entailed.

Of course, like any class, things did not always run to perfection. Somewhere around the beginning of the second half of the term, some of the fire went out of the students' in-class discussions for a few weeks. In part, I think this was because the readings for these weeks were longer and more complex than the previous ones. Some of the blame for this also falls on my own shoulders. I found that it is more important than usual to be very organized in a blended learning section—I got behind one week in the middle of the course, which threw us out of our usual rhythm and made us discuss a reading in the classroom before we had time to consider it online.

Still, even this dry patch was not an unmitigated disaster, for I found that even when their discussion lagged a bit, the advantages of a blended learning format still showed themselves.

I could use the valuable classroom time to supplement the discussions they were already having online, and I could also add further information about the readings, putting the weekly material in the context of the course's larger themes.

I do, indeed, need to improve my classroom management. Since we were only meeting roughly half the time as a traditional section, the blended learning environment is very unforgiving: every second has to tell, for there is just no time to waste. I see this as actually another advantage of the blended learning strategy—it lends a sense of urgency to our proceedings in the classroom, which I think the students are quick to pick up on. The result is a better focused, more productive time together. However, I have had to learn how to adjust my own teaching strategies since I have grown used to luxuriating in four hours of class time a week.

There were also some problems with one or two students getting confused and having a hard time understanding how to use the courseware and participate online. Online learning courses are plagued with such problems. Here, again, the advantages of a blended format revealed themselves. I saw these students regularly in the classroom and could reiterate and clarify my online instructions and, if need be, meet with students to show them how to use myCourses. (In fact, I brought my computer to class in order to give them a quick overview of how the system worked).

> "I found the blended learning experience to be an exciting and profitable one. It offers the student a lot of the flexibility of online learning—but with the chance to develop relationships with other students, maintain some human contact and meet with the instructor when they have questions."

In meeting with students, I did get some useful feedback to the effect that it would have been helpful to send them more specific feedback on their participation week by week. This could be managed by sending a brief message to every student with either a simple, low-stakes grade for the week (such as a number from 1 to 5), or perhaps adding one of a few standard messages I could cut and paste (for instance, something like, "your own posting was good, but you need to respond to the other students as well").

Conclusion

In summary, though I still have a lot to learn as an instructor and I am occasionally frustrated at the inadequacies of the myCourses software, I found the blended learning experience to be an exciting and profitable one. Such a course offers the student a lot of the flexibility of an online learning section—but with the chance to develop relationships with other students, maintain some human contact and meet with the instructor when they have questions. Unquestionably, the Internet provides a powerful tool for letting students ponder course material at their own speed and respond to others in a nonthreatening environment, but I hope we continue to value the unique advantages a classroom has to offer as well.

Postscript

Teaching a blended learning class was a deeply rewarding experience that has, I think, changed the way I teach my other sections.

At the most fundamental level, I think I have gained confidence in my ability to encourage student discussions. The blended format has shown me how, if they are given enough time, students can respond to challenging material with interesting and productive discussions. This has happened because the online courseware provides a tool that helps me, the instructor, as well as the students to reach our full potential. I feel comfortable in challenging them with material I might not have been willing to use before, and students gain a mechanism that allows them to respond to the course material in a timely and insightful fashion.

Sometimes I have taken the blended format wholesale and have adapted it to traditional classroom sections. For instance, I taught an honors seminar in which, though I did not eliminate any time in the classroom, I used weekly online discussion sections to supplement and introduce the classroom conversation. These were bright and motivated students who responded well to this extra challenge and, as a result, we investigated the course material far more deeply than in previous sections.

At other times my use of this model has been more selective, setting up an online discussion topic, for instance, only on a week in which we are covering a particularly complex or difficult work.

In addition to changing the way I engage the course material, my experience with blended learning has also encouraged me to use this technology more fully in my classroom sections.

For instance, when teaching a large, double section of an upper division course, I used our online courseware to help manage the small groups. These groups would sometimes meet during class to discuss works we were considering, but they were also responsible for giving a presentation to the rest of the class. I set up discussion topics for each group, and this worked really well as a way for the group members to share ideas and work (even when they could not get together), and it also gave me a convenient forum in which I could give them my feedback.

This feature of our courseware has also helped groups in other classes. For instance, in a much smaller class, students were able to use an online discussion forum as a way of sharing images about which they were giving presentations.

Finally, I have grown comfortable using the quiz feature of myCourses. This may seem like a small thing, but I think this feature is often overlooked, and I have found this an invaluable tool for not only my online classes, but my brick and mortar sections as well. This feature can actually free up time in class that would otherwise be wasted in administering various types of examination and it also does a superb job of giving students a running check on their progress.

Thomas Stone is a lecturer in the English department in the College of Liberal Arts.

Fabio Escobar Castelli
Ethics in the Information Age
Department of Philosophy
College of Liberal Arts
2004-2005 spring quarter

Objectives

The objectives of a blended course were always fairly clear to me, at least in my own mind: I wanted more intensive exploration of assigned readings. One of my laments as a teacher has always been that verbal discussions are not typically able to go beyond one or two surface points. This is understandable, given that verbal conversation is difficult to follow for many individuals, especially when it becomes relatively complex and involves 30 or more participants.

The written word, of course, has no such limitations. A student can look at a text and examine it an unlimited number of times before commenting on it. This makes the written word inherently more contemplative and careful. It was this element of intensity—the quality of the written word to lend itself to greater argumentative depth—that I wanted to capture with the blended course design.

One final word on objectives: the standard course objective for my classes (whether in applied ethics or any other philosophical area) is the construction and evaluation of arguments. Therefore, the development of a more intensive focus on the readings was aimed toward developing greater acuity in these two areas of argumentation. A student who successfully completes the course would have gained a greater understanding of how to construct and spot sound arguments, as well as those which might lack soundness and/or validity.

Method

Since the overall objective was to encourage students to delve deeper and more intensively into the readings, the online course elements would have to encourage reading and argument analysis. The thinking was as follows: if lectures are incapable of encouraging the depth of argumentative analysis that I am hoping for, then perhaps moving some of those tasks to the online realm will help achieve the goal.

With this in mind, then, I developed the following instructional week for the blended course:

- On Tuesdays, we did not meet. Students instead submitted questions about assigned readings. The questions were designed to encourage reading, of course, but also to develop a structure where the student's natural curiosity would take over

- On Thursdays, we met for our regular classroom-based sessions. I lectured on the assigned readings and attempt to address the various questions that students had asked in their Tuesday assignments

- On Sundays, students submitted arguments about the issues isolated during the previous five days. We collaboratively developed the issues that would form the foundation for their arguments and they then submitted these responses over the weekend

> *The objective of a blended course was always fairly clear to me: I wanted more intensive exploration of assigned readings. The outcome was a success. The level of argumentation was clearly better when compared to prior instances of the course.*

The overall objective, again, was encouraging an intensity of focus on a given cluster of issues and texts. Since each text would be considered on Tuesday, Thursday, and Sunday (and thus three distinct times), the approach I designed would hopefully lead students to have a greater familiarity with the issues, a stronger retention of course material over the long term and an improved understanding of the arguments in the field. All of this would contribute to a greater intensity of understanding vis-à-vis the argumentative focus of the course.

Results

From the standpoint of the original objective, the outcome was a success. The level of argumentation was clearly better when compared to prior instances of the course. While I regret not being able to supply non-anecdotal evidence to this effect, it is my personal impression that students were better able to understand the issues in the field and certainly more skilled in picking up the strategies of argumentation that are important to any applied ethics course. The arguments themselves had greater clarity and depth, they were researched better than in prior courses and students seemed to understand the issues better. In conclusion, therefore, I can state that all of the original pedagogical goals were met.

Postscript

Since participating in the Blended Pilot, I have continued to teach Ethics in the Information Age as a blended course and I have also added a new component that consists of self-paced, low-stakes, online quizzes. Three years of experience with the format and the course have not tempered my enthusiasm for its ability to generate better results than the traditional format.

What remains most valuable about blended learning is the following pair of pedagogical advantages:

1. It substantially increases the amount of writing that can be assigned

2. It makes significant course elements relatively self-paced, thus allowing students to take ownership of those elements

The writing component can be increased due to the fact that the feedback mechanisms are robust. Whether an instructor gives written or audio feedback to writing assignments, there is more time to read and meaningfully evaluate those assignments. Because there's no actual paper being exchanged between student and instructor, feedback can be given via an online setting in which most students are comfortable, thus creating a learning environment where they are able and willing to enthusiastically participate. The online environment also acts as a virtual organizer for students that might lack the organizational skills necessary for college success.

The self-pacing of the course allows students to learn material at their own pace. While some students will still choose to cram, the use of weekly low-stakes quizzing can encourage better learning by giving students the option of retaking quizzes multiple times. In effect, the quiz becomes a learning, rather than an assessment, tool. This technique pays dividends during finals time, since faculty can rely on the students' ownership of the course material to make the exam harder than in most courses. This self-paced element makes the student more keenly aware of his responsibilities for learning the material, thus improving learning.

Fabio Escobar Castelli is an adjunct instructor in the philosophy department in the College of Liberal Arts.

Christine Keiner

History of Women in Science and Engineering
Department of Science, Technology and Society
College of Liberal Arts
2004–2005 spring quarter

Objective

Prior to participating in the Blended Pilot, I had taught this course twice. Eliciting participation in the discussion sessions was a recurring frustration, with some students refusing to speak and others feeling the need to fill the gaps of silence by speaking too often. The positive comments of faculty members who had participated in the first year of the Blended Pilot encouraged me to investigate whether an asynchronous online discussion forum would increase the quality and quantity of student comments. The enrollment of several deaf and hard-of-hearings students, constituting 42 percent of the course, reinforced the need for a new discussion format.

Method

We met the first week for a regular in-class discussion; thereafter, for seven weeks of the course, I replaced 25 percent of the face-to-face classroom time with asynchronous online discussion sessions. I lectured one day a week (usually Tuesdays) and on the second day (usually Thursdays) met with the students for half the period to view and discuss films. On Wednesdays at noon, I posted a series of questions to the discussion area of myCourses. The students were required to choose and answer one of the questions by 6 p.m. that day, and to respond to the comments of at least one other student by 6 p.m. on Thursday. The initial comment had to be at least 150 words, and the second comment at least 100 words. As the instructions noted, "Comments must be substantive—in other words, you must support your opinions/interpretations/arguments with evidence from the readings."

To make this exercise work, I had to craft questions that would require students to integrate personal responses with supporting evidence from the readings. For example:

> According to historian Londa Schiebinger in her book *The Mind Has No Sex? Women in the Origins of Modern Science*, "It would be a mistake to think that [the eighteenth-century entomologist] Maria Merian was merely an exceptional woman who, defying convention, made her mark on science" (p. 79). Explain why you agree or disagree with this statement.

This week you read "The Place of Science in Woman's Education," a speech delivered in 1896 by Ellen Swallow Richards, a pioneer in the fields of public health, sanitary engineering and home economics. She argues that science education will actually help women become better wives and mothers, by teaching them proper ventilation, drainage, nutrition, psychology and other principles of "household management." After accusing women of lacking respect for the laws of nature, she asserts, "Science then should form an integral part of every woman's education, not merely because it will enable her to be a more efficient breadwinner... but because it is a corrective of certain grave faults which have grafted themselves upon her character" (pp. 225-226). Do you think that using stereotypes of bad housewives was a wise strategy to justify scientific education for women? If so, defend your response; if not, propose a different strategy for convincing Americans in the 1890s that all women needed to learn the principles of applied science.

Students were required to participate in all seven online discussions, and received a maximum of 30 points per discussion. The online discussion grades thus counted for 21 percent of the total points (1,000) for the course.

Since only 12 students registered, I did not divide them into separate online discussion sections. As a result, students had access to the posts of all of their peers.

Results

I was very pleased with the discussion outcomes, and believe the students appreciated the format. Midway through the course, I provided an extra-credit opportunity regarding the value of online discussions. Two of the responses follow:

> Online discussions allow students to think through their answers much more thoroughly before communicating them to the public arena. In class, the discussion proceeds rapidly and a student may be unable to follow or absorb all of the information. This could lead to a broken or "less educated" answer. The main advantage of the online discussion is the lack of time constraints. All the information can be read and a brainstorming session can occur [written by a hearing-impaired student].

> Face-to-face discussions have the benefit of moving through a broader range of topics...but the online discussions tend to have more depth, a greater equality of participation and the benefit of being their own notes and archive, the latter allowing an easy and comprehensive view of the course [written by a hearing student].

Other students noted the usefulness of having access to the readings during the dialogue, the comfort of expressing one's views in a less intimidating environment than the traditional classroom, and the leveling of the playing field for deaf, hard-of-hearing and hearing students.

"Face-to-face discussions have the benefit of moving through a broader range of topics...but the online discussions tend to have more depth."

I plan to continue using this method for this course since it did indeed improve the quality of student responses to assigned readings. One change I plan to implement is to require the students to focus their second response (i.e., the reply to another student's comments) on a different topic than their first response (i.e., the reply to my questions), in order to discourage "double-dipping." I might also require them to post at least three responses, rather than two, and to reduce the length requirement for the third response to 30-50 words. While most students did exceed the minimum number of required words per response, they rarely posted more than two responses. When they did, the discussions were more spirited. I look forward to experimenting with different response and word counts in the future.

Christine Keiner is an associate professor in the science, technology and society department in the College of Liberal Arts.

Babak Elahi
Immigrant Voices in American Literature
Department of English
College of Liberal Arts
2004-2005 spring quarter

Objectives

In blending Immigrant Voices in American Literature I hoped to do three things.

First, I wanted students to begin discussing the texts before they came to class. This would, I had hoped, take the classroom discussion to a higher intellectual level.

Secondly, I wanted students to have the option of keeping an online journal. The online journal would accomplish at least three pedagogical objectives: 1) it would allow students to keep a running log of their responses to the texts, 2) it would allow all students to read each other's journals (since these would be housed in public folders), 3) it would allow me to check on the journals frequently rather than collecting written journals every few weeks.

Finally, I wanted to encourage group activities, especially peer review of written assignments. These objectives tie directly into my teaching philosophy: a student-centered approach that emphasizes dialogue, active learning and interaction.

Method

During the first two weeks of the course, I introduced students to the course objectives, and made sure that all students had access to myCourses and were able to participate in the class online. In the third week, while I was away at a conference, we conducted all class discussion online. After this point, we substituted one online session for one class session each week, except for three weeks during which we met in class both days: I showed a film in class on a Thursday then we discussed it online over the weekend, and we met on Tuesday to discuss the film and the reading for that Tuesday.

More specific aspects of this method included the following:

1. Each week students responded to the reading in online journals (each "journal" was actually a one-person group in the myCourses discussion area). These journals were public, so that students could read and respond to each other's work. The public nature of these journals

also forced students to put more thought into each entry because they knew their peers would be reading them

2. On select weeks—especially in the second half of the quarter—students responded to each other in online discussions of readings and three films. This was, in some ways, merely an extension of the journals into a more direct dialogue with peers. This last use of myCourses allowed me to use class time to screen films and to utilize an asynchronous online structure for class discussion. Furthermore, one or two students each week were responsible for facilitating online discussion and reporting on the virtual discussion in the class meeting following any online session

> *"The online discussion primed the students for a higher level of intellectual engagement during class time. Students were coming to class with questions about, opinions on and critiques of the readings largely based on issues generated during online discussions."*

3. I split students up into groups of three or four to respond to each other's formal essays. These groups exchanged papers the week before papers were due and gave each other constructive criticism on those papers through the online format

Results

While some aspects of using a blended model worked well, others will require more structure and direction from me to be more effective in the future.

First, I will begin by reflecting on what went well and how to make sure I incorporate this aspect of my teaching into my next blended learning experience. Then, I will touch on those areas where students did not take full advantage of the online aspect of the course either for lack of involvement, for technical reasons or because I failed to encourage and enforce them enough. Finally, I will discuss how I can improve my own approach next time I teach a blended course.

First off, the online discussion did, indeed, prime the students for a higher level of intellectual engagement during class time. From the very beginning, students were coming to class with questions about, opinions on and critiques of the readings largely based on issues generated during online discussions. The online commentary often generated debates that might not have emerged in classroom only. Then, classroom discussion could reach a kind of meta-discourse in which we reflected on why certain debates emerged. The journals were especially useful, as they fulfilled more than one pedagogical purpose: they allowed individual exploration of the texts, they offered a kind of peer forum and they were a very effective means of evaluating each student's level (high or low) of participation in and engagement with the course.

There were some problems with this course. First, one student was unable to understand the course management system. I think I could have done more to help her use myCourses, but I think she was resistant to the very idea of a blended course. Second, the peer-review groups did not work out as expected, largely because I did not enforce peer-review group participation enough, but also because many students did not have their rough drafts ready on time. I will have to do more to enforce participation in the future, as well as the following:

1. I will be more attentive to individual student's difficulties logging on and using myCourses, even if they resist my help and involvement to some extent

2. I think I will return to in-class peer review sessions, and use online peer review as supplementary forums for feedback

3. I will gradually move to a fully online peer-review system as I provide more structure and attach more of a grade to these activities

4. In general, I think I can improve the effectiveness of the blended version of this and other courses by making more direct links between each individual activity and a specific grade or set of points

Babak Elahi is an associate professor in the English department in the College of Liberal Arts.

Richard Santana
Writing and Literature I
Department of English
College of Liberal Arts
2003–2004 winter quarter

Objectives

In blending this Writing and Literature course, one of the objectives was to get students to write in a lower-stakes setting. Writing Across the Curriculum (WAC) and Writing to Learn (WTL) strategies advise that students' engagement with writing can be deepened through protocols that ask students to write for purposes other than evaluation. Since half of the course was to be done online in a text-based environment, students were required to write under such conditions more often.

Another objective of blending the course was to increase interaction between students. In effect, reducing the face-to-face time represented an increase in "real writing" interaction among students. Students would have to communicate with each other and thus the purpose of their writing was to come to an understanding of the material rather than to achieve a high grade.

Method

I divided the course roughly in half into online and in-class time. We spent the first two weeks in traditional face-to-face setting and we did some practice myCourses exercises to establish familiarity with the technology and methods. From the third week on, we met once a week in the classroom and had an online activity in lieu of the other day. I was always available in chat sessions online on the days the class would have met. Students were encouraged, though not required, to attend the chat sessions. The purpose of the chat sessions was mainly to maintain interaction with the students and to answer questions about assignments. In general, about 50 to 60 percent of the students were in the general chat sessions.

The class was broken up into six permanent groups of four students. The online activities always involved some group work. Students read an assigned text and responded to a prompt, posting their response to the group. The members of the group then responded to their group mates and finally wrote a summary of the online discussion in their group, which they handed in at the following classroom meeting. In each case, I monitored the online discussions.

In addition to these structured online assignments, each group had the opportunity to get extra credit by meeting online and coming to a consensus on an assigned question about the text. For these meetings, I established individual chat rooms for each group. To get credit, the group had to log their discussion of the topic and come to an agreement. The extra credit questions were posted the day of the online meeting of the class. Students were thus encouraged to finish their assigned task before moving to the extra credit.

Results

The students responded really well to this method of instruction. Since I had just taught this same course with the same materials the previous quarter, I had a good opportunity for comparison. Part of what I wanted to accomplish was not to lose some of the impetus of the full time face-to-face model while creating more opportunities for writing and student interaction. This was successful in that students wrote about twice as much as they would have in an all face-to-face arrangement and interacted much more with their groups.

In these online discussions, I did not grade for grammar or language accuracy. The point of the exercise was for effective communication and engagement with ideas. As according to WAC and WTL protocols, students were encouraged to exchange ideas freely without being penalized for language errors. In the higher-stakes assignments, however, students were corrected and graded according to language rules and accuracy.

In a certain sense this created two levels of "blendedness" in this course. In their online activities, students were free to use language without correction. While this may seem counter-intuitive in a writing class, this exchange simulates what occurs in the traditional face-to-face classroom. However, there is the added bonus that the discussion takes place in writing rather than verbally. The discussions are written down and so form a record. Since the discussions were tied to the assigned (graded/ corrected/ high stakes) writing, this written record helped students develop their ideas more fully.

In comparison with their face-to-face cohorts, the papers in this course were more fully engaged with the ideas and ultimately more grammatically correct. Final grades in this course, as compared with my previous traditional course, were generally higher (there were 11 As, as opposed to six in the previous course).

Finally, in this course students wrote more, were more interactive with their classmates and ultimately wrote more engaged and more grammatically accurate papers, thus receiving higher grades overall.

Richard Santana is an assistant professor in the English department in the College of Liberal Arts.

Imaging Arts and Sciences

Jill Kepler
Design History Seminar
School of Design
College of Imaging Arts and Sciences
2004-2005 spring quarter

Objective

The Design History Seminar is a core graduate experience that explores the history of design. The seminar is one of three courses across the two-year curriculum, which allows students from the three distinct design disciplines (graphic design, industrial design and computer graphics design) to work together. The main objectives for blending this course include the following:

- Meet the critical need for student choice

- Encourage participation in discussions

- Increase the quality of discussions

- Increase the frequency of participation from international, learning disabled, and deaf and hard-of-hearing students

- Increase online communication skills

- Recognize the differences in using online communication tools in a professional environment as opposed to more informal interactions

- Enable students on the graduate level to teach each other

- Show students that learning can take place in various contexts

Method

The seminar class met two days out of the week. There was a two-hour lecture on Tuesday and a two-hour discussion session based on Tuesday's lecture on Wednesday. Two instructors taught the course on Tuesdays and the class was divided roughly in half on Wednesdays between the two instructors. The students had a choice to participate online or in-class for the Wednesday discussion session. The first Wednesday of the online discussion session was spent face-to-face.

Students were given specific goals and objectives for blended learning and were provided with a handout detailing the course expectations. Here are a few of the examples: sharing of student resources (i.e., attachments and URLs), effective integration of research, outside resources, information obtained through investigation, and effective communication and expression of lecture comprehension, inquiry, and knowledge.

Students were exposed to nine guest lecturers throughout the quarter on Tuesday evenings. The lecture topics and guest speaker information were posted in myCourses by date in the content area.

Every week, students who chose the online option were required to post two critical questions in the discussion board in preparation for the lecture before the following Tuesday. They were encouraged to conduct research on the subject that will be delivered to them in order to write a well thought out critical question.

> "Quite often students do not respond until after they have had some time to incubate, especially if they are apprehensive of a large face-to-face discussion. Sometimes their ideas are hatched outside of the in-class time."

There were also handouts posted online, i.e., "A Typology of Questions" and "How to Write a Critical Question" by R. Roger Remington. This helped students formulate their ideas into meaningful well-developed and educated questions. Students were not required to reply to the online prep questions on the discussion board, but may if they desired. These questions were intended for the students to use in class on Tuesday's lecture.

Every Wednesday, the students posted two critical response questions based on Tuesday's lecture in the appropriate weekly folder with the response notation by Wednesday at 6 p.m. They were encouraged to reply to four to five critical questions from other students in their discussion group every week.

All of the students in the Design History Seminar were required to write one critical essay and a case study. Students in the online portion of the Wednesday discussion group posted their case studies on the discussion board one week before they were due and had an assigned partner for critical feedback.

Results

Initially there was some confusion about assignments, such as where to post weekly questions, how to post weekly questions and which ones needed required responses. This was quickly resolved within the first week. I believe having an initial face-to-face meeting and a detailed handout helps the students get on track quickly.

With regards to students posting their case studies online, the students agreed that it was a great idea and eagerly participated. However, they felt that there was not enough time to gain feedback. Many students wished they had started their writing earlier and posted sooner.

Overall, I am pleased with the results of the online discussion group and feel that the students responded very well to this method of instruction. The design curriculum itself is a rigorous two-year 90-credit requirement. The students expressed an appreciation for having a choice to enroll in a blended course and felt that it was easier to manage their cumulative workload.

In previous quarters, the in-class discussion sessions were intended to create a dynamic dialogue with and between the students. However, every week the same few students spoke while others simply listened. Blended learning allows interaction independently of the class time, therefore allowing students to continue the in-class dialogue. I quickly noticed that the quality of postings tend to be higher than the in-class responses.

To quote one participant in the blended pilot program, "Quite often students do not respond until after they have had some time to incubate, especially if they are apprehensive of a large face-to-face discussion." Since half of the class is typically international and interdisciplinary, it is critical that the students benefit from each other. Blended learning allows other students to be exposed to these ideas whereas they may not have otherwise. "Sometimes their ideas are hatched outside of the in-class time."

Modifications

In the future there are a few things that I would change:

- More efficient organization of the weekly discussion boards

- Effective collaboration with the guest lecturers so the students can ask their critical prep questions during Tuesday's lecture

- Adding guest lecturers onto the discussion board the week after they present to answer questions. There is also the possibility of adding the guest lecturer on the board before they present, so that they may view questions the students may ask before they visit. This may provide the students with higher quality answers and meaningful elaborations. However, this may take an additional 20 minutes of the guest lecturer's time

- Require the students to post less critical prep and response questions as they draw close to their critical essays and case study writing assignments. Many of the students needed more help and feedback as they formulated a hypothesis for their case studies. As I graded their case studies, I found that some of them did not have a hypothesis, while others had a hypothesis that I had to dig for. The majority of the students whose hypothesis I had to dig for actually answered it. Overall, I see a potential for the online discussion tool to help the students formulate a solid hypothesis. The timing and balance simply needs to be better

> *"Technological skills will be highly favored for teachers in the 21st century. Today's students are diverse, busy, technically savvy and mobile."*

Again, I am pleased with the results. I feel that the objectives listed above were met and I would not hesitate to blend the course again.

Postscript

Since the Blended Pilot, I have taught at the college level for the University at Buffalo, again at RIT and am now a full-time faculty member at Roberts Wesleyan College.

My experience teaching a blended course at RIT has been very beneficial. Although I am not currently teaching a blended or online course, I am a second year member of the Instructional Technology Committee at Roberts Wesleyan College. Our goal for the new academic year is to increase online and blended learning across the curriculum.

Technological skills will be highly favored for teachers in the 21st century. Today's students are diverse, busy, technically savvy and mobile. As a whole, I am aware that educators tend to keep a tight rein on old ways of learning and processing information. My advice is simple—educators should aspire to keep current with technology and pay attention to how students think and process information. If you do this, you will likely measure up to student expectations.

Colleges must be able to appropriately identify which courses would be beneficial for blended and online learning. Some courses are suitable for online learning while others are more fruitful as face-to-face or blended. There are many factors involved, including college credits sold, current demand for courses, training, technology, assessment methods and faculty interest. Course quality is important. The college must have an effective course management system. Assuming technology is appropriate and the faculty member has been trained, their course may be well designed and poorly taught. Another example would be a course that is taught well and poorly designed.

Faculty should be open-minded and eager to create a new structure for teaching and learning. This takes time, patience and support from the college's information technology team. If a course doesn't initially succeed, this doesn't mean it's not suitable for blended or online learning. Instructors need to reflect, move the course forward and share knowledge with their colleagues. Effective course assessment is critical.

Jill Kepler is an assistant professor of graphic design in the Division of Art at Roberts Wesleyan College and an adjunct professor in RIT's College of Imaging Arts and Sciences.

Eileen Feeney Bushnell

Graduate Forum
School of Art
College of Imaging Arts and Sciences
2005-2006 fall quarter

Objectives

For the past five years, I have used online instructional technologies for the following reasons:

- To provide 24/7 access to course materials and assignments
- To more easily grade large populations of students

Over time, my ability to intuitively interact with these technologies has grown. Consequently, my reasons for offering Graduate Forum in a blended format were more complex, being centered on the exploration and discussion of course content.

One of the primary goals of this course is for students to contextualize their own desires, beliefs and processes in relationship to the various issues that underlie contemporary artistic practice. In blending Graduate Forum— that is, in incorporating online discussions into the course—students were given the opportunity to make connections between assigned readings, outside references, class presentations and class discussions. I hoped that this synthesis of sources would provide the informational means for students to more actively participate in class discussions.

The online format would provide a broad diversity of both source material and examples of peer research and review. I felt that this interactive discussion would also yield responsive writings that were well informed and personally meaningful. I hoped that blending the course would provide a model for the type of writing and discourse involved in the research and development of their graduate thesis.

Method

I divided the course into five basic components:

1. A weekly reading posted within the content section that addressed the issue to be discussed

2. A discussion section component, "Enhancing the Dialogue," that asked students to post some additional information that expands upon

their own understanding of the issues being discussed. This information could take the form of additional readings, criticism, popular culture, science, art, etc., quotes, images, maps, and so on

3. In-class presentation that was interactive and collaborative

4. In-class discussion that referenced all that had preceded it in relationship to the topic

5. A responsive writing component that asked students to place themselves in context to the issue that had been discussed. These responses should include references to all of the above, their impact on an each student's own work and processes and the citation of an artist's work that references their personal response to this topic

Results

The class discussed and voted to place all of the interactive components for the course in the public discussions section, so that all students would have access to each other's research and writing. Despite what I considered to be this terrific beginning, the initial response to the digital components of the class was disappointing. Being slightly older and deeply involved in the fine arts and crafts tradition, these students had, in general, less experience with anything digital. Several in-class presentations and a series of individual meetings the first few weeks helped most students become more technologically literate.

As a result of the slow start, the initial submissions to "Enhancing the Dialogue" were extremely brief and often overly autobiographical in nature. Still, students who were leaders in in-class discussions often wrote the most complex responsive writings. It took over five weeks for students to begin to respond to each other's writings and, again, verbal leaders in class became verbal leaders in online discussion.

Once students became used to the online format, however, they became more responsive to the submissions of their classmates, more interactive in terms of classroom dialogue and the quality of responses increased significantly. I think that, overall, once students began to use the online components as a reference, their ability to write about and discuss issues advanced considerably.

Modifications

Having moved through Graduate Forum as a blended course, there are a number of things that I will change in the future. These include:

- Incorporate letter grades. In the past, I have resisted using letter grades for the various components of the course. Having observed the resistance to the digital interactions, I feel that students in this class would benefit from the incentive of letter grades to encourage participation

- Incorporate the use of pairs or groups of students to work on the writing components of the class. This will force students to more carefully read the work of their classmates and allow them to more carefully consider the components of each response

- Incorporate Pachyderm (an application for hyper linking image, text and audio files) as a means of providing visual images as online references for writing

- Incorporate Pachyderm as a means of allowing students to create responses that are both visual and verbal

- Incorporate a more interactive approach to content through the use of the dropbox. I have begun to use the dropbox as a site to collect visual information relating to content. Students answered questions or requests by finding visual references that were submitted as digital files. I, in turn, used these images to create PowerPoint presentations that became initial points of discussion for the exploration and interpretation of conceptual issues. The process reinforces each issue by contextualizing the ways in which students already know or experience information. I hope to incorporate this approach within Graduate Forum

> *"This approach enhanced the understanding content, the depth and breadth of in class discussions and an overall improvement in the quality of the writing."*

Conclusion

One of the primary reasons that I desired to participate in this blended learning initiative was to enhance the verbal and written responses to the content of this course. This approach allowed me to expand the content each student was receiving outside of the required course materials and to provide a number of models on which to base their responses, by allowing them access to each other's writings. Inevitably, this approach enhanced the understanding content, the depth and breadth of in class discussions and an overall improvement in the quality of the writing.

Postscript

In the year following my initial interaction with the blended learning format, I expanded the use of the digital interactive components in an effort to deal with content from a number of different directions.

In addition to the original five components of the course, I created student discussion groups to review the reading and submit a synopsis of critical information in the discussion section. A rotating weekly leader is responsible for the collection and synthesis of the information.

The class once again voted to post all information generated in reviewing the articles before class in the discussions section. This made all submitted work available to all students and again generated limited self-referential dialogue among participants. More significantly, I assigned letter grades to these submissions, which quickly clarified the expected substance and quality. The creation of discussion groups around the assigned readings had the more significant result of preparing students to a much greater degree for in-class discussions. Students were more informed and confident—even opinionated—as a direct result of this initiative and in-class discussions grew increasingly interactive.

The creation of discussion groups also afforded the opportunity to reserve one group for foreign students for whom English is a second language. With financial support from my department chair, I was able to assign a graduate student who had previously taken the course to the group to help facilitate understanding and answer questions about the reading.

Despite a clear understanding on my part that this type of enhancement was needed for the ESL students, the assignment of these students to a single section was met with resistance to what they felt was their isolation from the rest of the class. Once these students began to meet as group, however, the advantages and the benefits of this structure became clear. This format allowed ESL students to take control of the group without any worries about language difficulties and empowered group members to take on the rotation leadership role, a result that I had originally anticipated would fall to the assisting graduate student. These students were able to approach class discussions with an expanded knowledge of the content involved and a greater sense of confidence in their ability to participate. In particular, this approach encouraged the women of this group, normally reticent participants in classroom discussions, to become more active participants.

A subsidiary but significant response to this structured discussion section was that a number of students with learning disabilities asked to join the group in order to take advantage of the added support.

For the "Enhancing the Dialogue" component, students were, to a greater degree, encouraged to submit responses that were digital and visual in form. This directional emphasis was a response to presentations involving visual sources of inspiration that many students in our college are required to construct as an aspect of their thesis preparation and the growing enmeshment of the arts and the Internet. The student response to this initiative was tremendous and resulted in an information source for the entire class that included links to galleries, museums and individual artist's websites as well as digital photographs of exhibitions that individual students had attended. Students continued to have the opportunity to submit related readings, but the emphasis on a visual response created a significantly more interactive repository of information.

My desire to implement Pachyderm as a means of providing visual images as online references for writing and solutions in and of themselves was subverted by a sabbatical whose goals embraced the growth and enhancement of my own artwork. In reference to ideation and problem solving, the implementation of this application continues to be a significant objective in the growth and development of my curriculum.

Eileen Feeney Bushnell is an associate professor in the School of Art in the College of Imaging Arts and Sciences.

Michael Kleper
New Media Publishing
School of Print Media
College of Imaging Arts and Sciences
2004-2005 winter quarter

Method

In designing this course in a blended format, I reduced seat time by half and divided the class into small groups that remained intact throughout the quarter. I tried to have weekly activities that involved both group and individual components—and allowed small groups to operate flexibly, rotating group leaders and making decisions on their meeting times and modes of communication, their approach to assignments and other elements.

I saw group dynamics at work by viewing some of their online discussion transcripts and heard during class how some of the groups were interacting. Although the groups might have had some minor difficulties—in scheduling, getting full participation, etc.—no one reported any problems to me and all groups met all of their responsibilities, if not all of their deadlines. In one instance, I felt that none of the groups had completed an assignment satisfactorily and had been rather lazy about it. I required them to redo it and they all did a much better job. I think that those assignments which followed were taken a bit more seriously.

One of the aspects that I felt was most beneficial was the number and variety of activities that enabled students to visit environments outside the confines of the college and to meet individuals who they would not otherwise have been exposed to. They were able, for example, to tour the RIT HUB and analyze their digital workflow and get a first hand look at Xerox's new iGen3 digital press in Webster. They were able, through a web conferencing meeting using Macromedia Breeze (now Adobe Connect), to interact with one of the leading experts in the field who writes research reports on the subject under study and who, coincidentally, is an RIT graduate of the School of Print Media. A wonderful role model to be sure!

I have been encouraged by the creativity I have seen in some of the group work and in the quality of some of the online discussion contributions. Giving students the freedom and flexibility to manage their time commitment and work outside of the classroom walls seems to be an effective means of creatively enhancing a course.

With only one lecture per week—rather than two—I believe that the content presented was more comprehensive. Certainly nothing was lost by redesigning the course in a blended format and, I believe, much was gained. I rewrote or revised all of the lectures and, in most cases, had two weekly PowerPoint presentations, one of the lecture material and the other of the blended learning activities. I provided students with PDF files of both, via myCourses, every week. These files were always provided in advance of our meeting so that students could read them, print them, take notes on them and be prepared to ask questions.

"The blended experience provided the means to present a more interesting and interactive course. Both the students' and my time was spent more efficiently and produced a more meaningful and enjoyable end result."

Conclusion

In summary, the blended experience provided the means to present a more interesting and interactive course. Both the students' and my time was spent more efficiently and produced a more meaningful and enjoyable end result.

The blended dimension allows a new degree of freedom in creating activities that are beyond the traditional lecture format. I felt empowered with options that were never feasible within the time constraints of standard scheduling.

Michael Kleper is a professor emeritus in the School of Print Media in the College of Imaging Arts and Sciences.

Bob Chung

Tone and Color Analysis
School of Print Media
College of Imaging Arts and Sciences
2003-2004 winter quarter

Background

I teach color-imaging aspects of digital media as they apply to print and publishing. Using digital communication technologies, such as myCourses and the Internet, to support my teaching makes perfect sense. I have previously taught online courses for more than four years. I was able to convert much of my course materials in the form of digital media, e.g., PDFs of PowerPoint handouts, streamed videos of lectures and lab demos, self-quizzes with questions randomly pulled from a test bank, etc.

Utilizing these digital resources for campus courses seemed to be the next step in my evolution as a teacher. An immediate benefit is that these resources do not make face-to-face meetings a requirement for learning.

Objectives

I offered Tone and Color Analysis to 15 graduate students in a blended format on campus. This was a required course with nine international students and one deaf student attending.

One goal of blended learning is to replace face-to-face instruction with more student-to-student interactions. In this instance, the instructor becomes a facilitator and myCourses becomes the virtual meeting place with discussion boards posting and various student-generated notes.

Method

Effective blended learning requires a different strategy than teaching as usual. I received assistance from Online Learning before the beginning of the quarter—in setting up heterogeneous groups at the beginning of the quarter, learning to use myCourses and warm-up exercises.

This was a four-credit course. The class met two three-hour blocks a week. I decided to lecture only three hours a week and used streamed video to pick up the slack. The other three hours were allotted to the lab component of this course.

I divided the class into five groups of three and asked each group to approach each lab assignment as a group project. I met with the class and gave unannounced quizzes at the beginning of the lab session to assure good attendance. I then answered questions pertaining to specifics of a lab assignment. The class was dismissed to allow small groups to interact afterwards.

Students were grade conscious. There were two closed-book tests accounting for 50 percent of the grade, four lab assignments accounting for 40 percent of the grade, and 10 percent for unannounced quizzes.

Having small group interaction was not an easy task. Having small group interaction documented with the use of myCourses was harder for my students. I had to introduce new rules, e.g., minimum postings per week per person for lab grading.

Results

The blended course was a success to me and to my students. Instead of procrastinating on lab assignments, small lab groups tackled the project head on without delay. The lab report submitted as a group produced higher quality than individual reports. Students who were more capable would lead. The group that produced the best report for an assignment was recognized in front of their peers and their work, in the form of a PDF file, made available to the entire class. I was viewed more like an advisor or a coach as opposed to an adversary. There were more As in the class than in previous classes.

In hindsight, a number of factors made my blended learning journey a very positive experience; these include:

- Readiness of coursework in digital media (not sure if it works equally well for a junior faculty member)

- Maturity of graduate students (not sure if it works for undergraduate students who are much younger)

- Course content is imaging- and computing-intensive, and the class size is small (not sure if it works for liberal arts class with large number of students)

The future of blended learning at RIT looks good from what I can see. Students may adopt blended learning easier than faculty members. Getting faculty involved with more pilot programs is recommended as we continue the journey toward active learning in all courses.

Bob Chung is a professor in the School of Print Media in the College of Imaging Arts and Sciences.

Nicole Cox
Western Art and Architecture
School of Art
College of Imaging Arts and Sciences
2004-2005 fall, winter, and spring quarters

Objective

My objective in blending this course was to engender more and better discussions in response to additional—outside of the assigned text—readings. Typically, during the class time I'd allot for these discussions, the same handful of people would contribute, and the majority of students would sit mutely by, either not confident enough or unsure about how to participate.

One of my goals in using the blended model was for students to become more involved with the material, making connections between outside readings, class lecture and other outside sources (e.g., classes and readings seemingly unrelated to the material of this course)—pulling these sources together and "teaching" their fellow group members about what it is they all just read and how it applies to the bigger picture. I had hoped that through this interactive discussion, writing a response paper would move from the realm of an esoteric exercise into global conversation production.

An added benefit of this model is that students would write more and so get more experience in organizing and expressing ideas in writing—a skill which can be lost if not practiced.

Method

I divided the class into online discussion groups of four to six people. Students posted their responses to the readings online within their own group and then had the opportunity to read the responses from their teammates. Once they'd read all the responses within their group, they were asked to write a reaction to at least one other response.

I saw my role as that of a moderator. I jumped in when necessary to keep the conversations on track, gently nudging a group along if they seemed to lose focus or miss the point of the reading. My ultimate goal here, however, was to not have to prod the conversation along, but to allow the students to lead their own groups and discussions.

Seat time that would have otherwise been reserved for discussions regarding the additional readings was reduced (approximately 15 minutes) for each paper. Each response and reaction combined was worth 5 percent of the student grade (3.5 percent for the initial response, 1.5 percent for the reaction.)

Results

Survey of Western Art and Architecture is a three-quarter required course taught sequentially over the academic year, and most students remain in the same section through the academic year. This offered me a unique opportunity to get a sense of the impact that online discussion would have when consistently facilitated over the course of a year.

> "There was a definite improvement in writing skills—I think they taught each other. Using proper grammar and a more academic tone to make a point somehow makes it seem more valid than one made in all lowercase colloquialisms."

Fall quarter responses, especially the very first ones, were very much what I had come to expect in the traditional or non-blended format. Students turned in responses that were literal in their interpretation of the readings, response formulation was done from a more egocentric point of view and the writing, when bad, was really bad. Consequently, I needed to spend a lot of time in the discussion groups, moving conversations along, bringing up missed points and, at times, addressing inappropriate comments (these issues were addressed offline in private meetings in my office.) I think the students were a bit reticent at first to question each other and would often make superficial, subjective (and often, blandly positive) comments about each other's responses. As the fall quarter moved on, and students began to get the hang of it—I didn't need to be such a micro-manager (either online or in class, "C'mon guys *say* something [substantive]!")

By the end of the winter quarter, and more obviously during the spring quarter, there was a remarkable shift in the discussions. The students within the groups were talking to each other, not at me or at the authors of the readings. In responding to other postings within their groups, they would write things like, "I never thought of that before..." "Although I see your point, I think you're forgetting..." or "What the author really meant was..."

There was also a definite improvement in writing skills—again, I think they taught each other. Most groups had at least one student whose writing was actually quite polished (both in content and style), and they would sort of lead by example. Using proper grammar and a more academic tone to make a point somehow makes it seem more valid than one made in all lowercase colloquialisms. I also think a form of peer pressure forced students into more vigorous participation. Students whose work was not on par with the work of the other members of the group would sometimes be shunned—left out of the discussion. As participation was an important part of a student's grade, those students soon learned the level of acceptable production in order to be considered a viable member of the group.

Overall, I think the blended model helped make the students become better learners. Evidenced in both their online discussions and in-class participation, they were able to make connections between knowledge gathered from one reading to the next, from lecture to reading (and visa versa) and from personal experiences outside this class throughout. Students had a better understanding of the material they were studying as well as the platform on which it is presented. Not one student failed the course and the highest grades by incidence were As and Bs. (And anecdotally, I don't think "Easy Grader" is the first—or even fifth—term that students would use to describe me.)

Modifications

Although it was my ultimate goal to not appear in the online conversations, I think the students would have liked more interaction. I would often talk to groups in class about this or that point they had made, but I think doing it online within their discussion group would have give them immediate feedback and offered greater affirmation of their work.

For more student involvement, instead of the instructor creating a list of questions or talking points for each specific reading, I think, in the future, I would assign a rotating pair of students within each group to post those queries. Doing it this way would require more in-depth and intimate involvement from the instructor to come up with viable ideas—and, of course, could still be done online, maybe even in real-time, to allow for freer brain-storming.

I would carve out a definite, posted and planned, chunk of seat time to make up for the significant amount of time that students spend online in their discussion groups. I may have asked for a little too much time from these students but, really, they rose to the occasion.

Conclusion

One of the main reasons I incorporated the blended model into this survey art history course sequence was to have more students participate in discussions. I thought that creating a somewhat anonymous environment for them to do so could help those students who were less confident speaking in public. In the end, this objective proved itself quite nicely. The students who were normally classroom participators were also confident in their online presentations (as was to be expected) and were not shy about sharing their opinions, voicing disagreement or even taking charge of a discussion's direction. The real benefit of the online discussion was evident in the participation of the "other" student. (For the sake of this evaluation—there are two types of students: the good student, but quiet, not needing or wanting to make a "show" of their

"A form of peer pressure forced students into more vigorous participation. Students whose work was not on par would sometimes be shunned–left out of the discussion. They soon learned the level of acceptable production in order to be considered a viable member of the group."

knowledge accumulation in class {Type A}; and the average to below-average student who's not sure about why they are taking this course and has a more difficult time understanding the material {Type B}.)

Type A students were able to shine online. Free from the stress of public performance, they were able to clearly and articulately voice a point of view, and bandy ideas about with other members of the group.

Type B students were given an opportunity to understand the material from several different points of view and, importantly, from peers whose experiences were more similar to their own. For some, hearing it from a peer can make a point seem more valid than hearing it from someone who seems to have ages ago bought the whole theory hook, line and sinker and lives a life far removed from the day-to-day realities of an undergraduate student. These students are also offered the opportunity to put their own ideas forward and have them affirmed within a pretty supportive environment or have themselves gently (ideally) nudged from their original point of view to a more carefully considered conclusion, again by their peers.

Basing the results on my original objective, I would say that, in general, blending this course was a success. It is a model that I would, in an amended form, repeat in subsequent survey courses; and I would look for ways to incorporate it into other Art History or even studio practicum—like Creative Sources—classes.

Postscript

I left RIT for a teaching position at the State University of New York at Geneseo the year after I participated in the Blended Pilot. At the time,

SUNY Geneseo was not set up to practically run a blended course, and this turned out to be a great disappointment to me. I had an even greater number of students in my classes at SUNY Geneseo—upwards of 125 per class—making real-time, in-class participation very difficult to manage. I think those students missed out on an important opportunity to participate with their peers about the subject matter in the same meaningful way as the students in the RIT blended courses.

After two years at SUNY Geneseo, I decided to finally pursue that career in science I put off many years ago. I am currently a full-time student in the Physician Assistant program at RIT. Three years after participating in the Blended Pilot, I am keenly aware of the ubiquitous online component for each of my classes. Most of the faculty members I've taken classes with move some portion of their classes online ,even if it's just to list homework assignments and grades. I am amazed at how quickly this novel idea became a normal and natural tool in current teaching practice.

Nicole Cox is currently a full-time student in the Physician Assistant program at RIT.

Science and Engineering

Richard Doolittle
Anatomy and Physiology I
Department of Medical Sciences
College of Science
2004-2005 fall quarter

Background

The two-quarter sequence in Anatomy and Physiology is a required set of courses for a number of majors both within and outside of the College of Science. In the past, the course has included four hours of lecture and three hours of laboratory exercises per week. Historically, class enrollment has averaged around 40-50 students but, in recent years, has grown significantly to more than 100 students with a diverse set of goals, expectations and levels of preparedness.

As a content-heavy class, students are asked to learn a large volume of information, mainly through lecture delivery, by simply attending class. Because of the class size and lecture-based format, it was hard—if not impossible—to determine individual student competency level other than by formal written examinations. All of the exams were multiple choice/matching, computer-graded exercises. There was little opportunity, given this structure for lecture, to get to know the students and to engage them in productive discussions.

Objectives

In an attempt to create a more productive learning environment for students, a new approach was created to achieve the following goals and objectives:

- Provide more insight into individual student comprehension and mastery of material

- Create group dynamics that encourage student discussions outside of lecture and lab, i.e., create small active learning communities

- Provide students the incentive and motivation to learn basics by asking provocative questions about medical applications

- Help students develop skills of oral communication

- Enhance the student/faculty relationship to increase the interactions and potential learning experiences between student and instructor

- Reduce the amount of lecture seat time
- Make use of myCourses to enhance exchange of information
- Create more opportunities for review-based recitation sessions
- Reduce stress that comes with multiple lab practical examinations proven to be of little use in stimulating learning

"The amount of time invested in this initial experiment proved to be an important step in changing my overall philosophical approach toward teaching science and helping to mentor others on how best to manage pedagogical change."

Method

The class was broken down into three modules of information. Within each module, there were:

- Content-based lectures (all PowerPoint, posted in myCourses)
- Concomitant lab exercises
- One week with no lectures (replaced by non-mandatory review sessions)
- Lab discussion days with six student group presentations
- A culminating lecture examination

Discussion groups

Students within each laboratory group (no more than 24 students) were randomly assigned to a group of three to four students per group. Specific "problem" assignments were announced during the first laboratory period. Students were then given 10 minutes to gather in their respective groups, introduce themselves to each other and come up with a name for their group (named after a bone or bony landmark).

Groups were then randomly assigned a number between one and six that would correspond to their question/problem number throughout the quarter. Random assignments were also made for the order of presentation within each group (using playing cards). Presentations were limited to 10-12 minutes with a 10-minute question and answer period to follow. All members of the group were allowed to participate in the Q-and-A in providing appropriate responses. In each case, students were to work as a group in the preparation of PowerPoint slides and accompanying text. For each presentation, students were graded as a group and, where appropriate, as an individual (given either unsatisfactory or excellent performance) on content and quality of presentation. I attended all lab sections and evaluated presentations (30 presentations/module). Students were also asked to provide feedback and a numerical grade for each group as well. Information was collated and grades posted within myCourses. This exercise accounted for 30 percent of the overall course grade.

Conclusions

This pilot made me nervous on a number of fronts. Firstly, the discipline of anatomy and physiology is a content-heavy course that serves as a foundation for a wide variety of majors. The demographic of the class was quite unique with physician assistant, biology, premed, nutrition and engineering students, to name just a few.

In moving to a blended approach, there was a 30 percent reduction in lecture hours (reduced from 40 to 28 lecture hours). I found more opportunities, however, to teach more effectively within the guise of the student PowerPoint presentations and ensuing discussion/review periods. Additionally, the four hours of available lecture time per module fell during the week before the examination, which turned into productive non-mandatory review sessions for those needing the extra help.

I was also a bit hesitant in asking students to organize themselves into groups and be prepared for their first oral presentation a mere three weeks into the quarter. Much to my surprise and to their credit, students organized quickly and efficiently in time to make exceptional presentations. Much of this effort reflects the predominance of "type A" personalities within the class; particularly within the ranks of the electrical engineer and physician assistant students.

Although this pilot was demanding on my time, I felt I got to know each and every student in the class through direct interactions—in person and online. I might alter the course to reduce the overall number of presentations but, clearly, the students thrived in this new approach as evidenced by the positive evaluation feedback and overall increase in mean examination average.

Postscript

The greatest lesson I learned from the Blended Pilot came from taking a risk and a giant leap of faith into the unknown and unchartered waters of untested teaching methodologies.

The amount of time invested in this initial experiment proved to be an important step in changing my overall philosophical approach toward teaching science and helping to mentor others on how best to manage pedagogical change.

It's been several years since this initial project, but nearly all aspects of my current course offerings have been changed to encourage more student-student interaction and problem-solving approaches to enhance the learning environment and invest students directly in the learning process on a class-by-class basis—all while reducing the total amount of time I spend in front of the class simply talking at them.

Time spent on the Blended Pilot, and later in conference with colleagues as part of the RIT Faculty Learning Community, has presented fabulous (and almost unlimited) access to new approaches in how to help my students. These experiences helped to reinvigorate my passion for teaching in higher education and opened my mind and future to fresh ideas.

Richard Doolittle is a professor and chair of the department of medical sciences in the College of Science.

Paul Craig
Biochemistry Conformation and Dynamics
Department of Chemistry
College of Science
2004–2005 fall quarter

Objectives

I started teaching at RIT 12 years ago, confident that students learn more when the learning is participatory. On arriving, I found that there was a great deal of content that needed to be covered in my biochemistry courses to prepare students for the next step in their careers, which frequently involve either graduate or professional school. I resorted to a lecture style most of the time, but still wanted to find a way to make the class more interactive—to make the students more responsible for their learning. I entered the Blended Learning Pilot with the hope of doing just that.

Method

Class

Biochemistry Conformation and Dynamics is the first of three biochemistry courses in our yearlong sequence—it is followed by Metabolism and Nucleic Acids, then Molecular Genetics. This course covers topics ranging from water and amino acids to protein structure and the function of membranes in biological systems. This material is found in the first 13 chapters of the textbook, *Biochemistry*, 5th edition, by Jeremy M. Berg, Lubert Stryer and John L. Tymoczko.

Time

The class was scheduled to meet twice a week for 80 minutes. In the blended format, four of these class sessions were replaced with online discussions on the course weblog.

Content

Rather than simply have students rehash the textbook materials online (or find friends who were taking the fully online version of the same course so they could watch the pre-recorded lectures), I reduced the amount of material that I covered during regular class time and challenged students with a series of questions based on the current literature or on historical topics that are not covered in the text. Each of the four online discussions was worth 25 points. In total, this constituted 20 percent of the course grade. Grading was based on students making a conscientious effort, which they all did, so most of them received all 100 points.

> *"Students frequently posted more than they were required to. I wonder if this resulted from the fact that they were meeting face-to-face as well as online, so that there was a level of friendship or collegiality."*

- Discussion 1: Students had to select one of three topics and post their own comments based on online resources and peer-reviewed literature, which they were required to cite (20 points). They also had to reply to someone else's comment in any of the three areas (5 points)

- Discussion 2: From discussion 1, I realized that not everyone had read all three topics, since they could post their comments and respond within a single topic. For the second discussion, they were required to post a comment on one of two topics, and then post a reply to someone else's comments in each of the topics

- Discussion 3: This course also includes a protein project wherein students are required to prepare animations of the protein structure using a software tool called BioEditor. For this discussion, all the students had to read a recent paper from the literature on a unique protein structure. They then had to post code that would create an informative animation of that structure

- Discussion 4: I returned to the approach described in discussion 2 (post your own comment on one of two topics and reply to someone else's comments on each of the two topics)

Results

I can identify two major outcomes in the teaching and learning process, both of which delighted me.

Covering new materials

In previous years, I used two methods to see if students could apply the concepts from the course to topics outside the course—projects where they had to read the literature and exam questions where they had to speculate on topics that were not covered in lecture. Both of these have drawbacks—for the projects (especially in a class of 30 or more students), it's hard for me to tell what they're really learning and what they're paraphrasing without much knowledge. For the exams, there's a lot of stress and frustration for students. By introducing new topics in an online discussion format, students were required to write thoughtfully about something they had not encountered before. It was less stressful than an exam or a project.

Students taught each other

This was the best part. I have used online threaded discussions in the past in fully online courses, and they were pretty flat—students completed what they had to and that was it. In the blog setting, students frequently posted more than they were required to. I wonder if this resulted from the fact that they were meeting face-to-face as well as online, so that there was a level of friendship or collegiality.

Conclusion

This was a very rewarding experience for me in that I was able to see students learn and apply that learning. The blended format with its online component afforded less pressure than an exam, but there was still the pressure of keeping up. And I told the students I expected them to read the textbook, even if we did not cover certain sections in class.

Postscript

I have long been an advocate of using online resources in my teaching. My participation with blended learning reinforced this approach and encouraged me to actually replace in-class time with online exercises and interactions.

Since that time, I have increased my use of online discussions in all of my courses. In these discussions, students are given a topic and are required to find a resource in the primary literature about that topic, then report their findings in a discussion format. They are then required to read articles that others have posted and make at least one comment on someone else's post.

I originally used the blended learning approach for one of my biochemistry courses, which is a required course for students majoring in biochemistry, biotechnology and bioinformatics. The students did not like the blended approach in this setting. They wanted to be able to ask me questions directly about the problems that we covered and did not feel like that worked for them in the blended format.

However, I have been using blended learning for my Chemical Literature course, where students learn to find, cite, read and present scientific literature. This is a two credit hour course, so that means 20 class meetings over the 10 week quarter in a traditional format.

I have used a blended format in this course for the last two years, where we meet face-to-face 12 or 13 times. During class meetings, we spend time discussing course materials and helping students find articles to present. The students then spend out-of-class time on a series of exercises relating to their scientific articles. They also spend out-of-class time going through online tutorials for our literature searching tools such as World of Science and PubMed. In addition, they work through online resources about plagiarism and complete a number of discussions that relate to evaluating the quality of scientific information, particularly on websites that are not peer-reviewed. They also spend out-of-class time preparing PowerPoint presentations and poster sessions, using guidelines that are discussed in class and can also be found on myCourses.

During my original blended course, I used a blog and had students register and participate in the blog. They learned a great deal and by the end of the quarter were actively teaching each other. It was a terrific learning experience for all of us, but it was also a lot of work for me, since I had to build the blog using Movable Type. I have since stopped using the blog and have chosen to use the discussion tool in myCourses.

Overall, I appreciated the suggestions from the Online Learning department on using blended methods and will use it in formats where the content is flexible (such as chemical literature), but plan to stick with traditional classroom learning in my content-rich courses, particularly in courses that are early in a sequence.

Paul Craig is a professor in the chemistry department in the College of Science.

Tim Gilbert
Math Thought and Processes
Center for Multidisciplinary Studies
College of Applied Science and Technology
2005-2006 winter quarter

Objectives

The objectives of the course are knowledge and skill based.

First, the student will receive knowledge of the principles of fundamental mathematics and algebra. Then algebraic notation and operational practices will be introduced with homework assignments aimed at skill building.

When the student has completed the course, he/she will be able to:

- Apply the fundamental properties of mathematics to the addition, subtraction, multiplication and division to numerals and variable

- Solve equations with one variable applying the rule of equality for equations relative to addition, subtraction, multiplication and division

- Construct and solve inequalities and graph their solutions

- Apply the rules of exponents for multiplication, division, addition and subtraction

My objective for blending the course was to expand students' skill level through group discussions and team problem solving. In the past, a few students usually dominated in-class participation. The students who participated were either the strongest students demonstrating their knowledge or the weakest students needing in-depth/remedial coaching. The middle ground of students who didn't need remedial help yet wanted to understand the subject matter more deeply were left out.

A goal of adopting the blended model was to draw out this middle ground of student. By having these students interact with each other online, along with the stronger and weakest students, they would develop better skills and a broader understanding of the topic.

An added benefit is that students would experience problems a second time by working on them together. These online discussions would be focused on the more complex examples from the in-class sessions and or the more complex homework problems.

Method

I divided the class into five equal-sized online study groups of four each. Through a note card query in class, I assessed the competence levels of the students. I then balanced their competencies across each of the groups. I instructed the students that participation in the groups would be rewarded by a five-point increase in their mid-term exam score. A condition of the increase was that all members of the group had to achieve an 85 or better on the exam.

"By having the middle-ground students interact with each other online, along with the stronger and weakest students, they would develop better skills and a broader understanding of the topic"

I then demonstrated that discussions on problems had to display calculations and note the algebraic rules and operations that were being applied.

For example:

$x+5 = 20$
$x+5+(-5)=20+(-5)$ (additive rule of equality and addition of the opposites)
$x=15$

The students were to also note the examples and pages from the text or companion CD that demonstrated the particular concepts they were working with.

Results

Participation levels of the students stratified by age and expertise. Younger students with higher math skills tended not to participate. Mature, non-traditional students participated and engaged in strong problem solving sessions. They not only exchanged calculations, they offered their unique perspectives on how problems should be solved. In one or two exceptions, younger advanced students joined in the discussions. Their participation enriched the discussions as they would note where the techniques would be helpful in other courses.

Modifications

Next time, I will assign online problems that must be worked by the group. The assignment will have an online and an in-class component.

I will have an online problem for each member of the group to be responsible for and require each person to lead their group online in a review of the problem. The source for these problems can be found at a section at the end of each assignment. These sections have more advanced problems that extend and deepen skills for each concept.

I will assess and give feedback to the group on a weekly basis in class. I will expect each group to lead an in-class review of their assigned problems. With a group assignment, if one or more problems are intractable, the group can bring that area of learning to the classroom discussion. If the problems are completed by the group, the class time can be utilized to review and reinforce the concepts and areas of skill development.

Tim Gilbert is an adjunct instructor for the Center for Multidisciplinary Studies in the College of Applied Science and Technology.

Spencer Seung Kim
Plastics Processing Technology
Manufacturing and Mechanical Engineering Technology/Packaging Science
College of Applied Science and Technology
2004–2005 winter quarter

Background

In the engineering and engineering technology community, we continuously strive to improve the education we provide for our students. The larger education community constantly shares with us new teaching and learning strategies, such as ones known to be effective for diverse learners. Underlying many strategies is a recognition and desire to be more learner-centered in our practices. Blended learning is one of these new strategies that RIT faculty are able to use within and outside the classroom to create engaging, leaner-centered forms of teaching and learning.

Plastics Processing Technology provides fundamentals in plastics processing to upper-level students. This course also tries to emphasize skill and knowledge needed in engineering tasks such as team work and problem solving for manufacturing plastic products. Keeping students engaged and on task in evening courses is a challenge. One of the most challenging aspects of teaching is trying to reach students who appear to be unmotivated in learning. This class meets Monday and Wednesday from 6 to 8 p.m. In the class, the students have different levels of motivation and different attitudes about learning. They also have differences to specific class environment and instructional practice.

Method

In the blended format of the course, I cancelled the Wednesday sessions (not the first and last sessions though) and substituted several online activities. The asynchronous online discussions were broken into small groups of three students; each group worked together in their online discussion boards for the duration of the quarter.

In the online discussions, I assigned discussion questions related to topics in the chapters of textbook. I also assigned two research projects that asked students to respond to specific questions in problem-solving in plastics processing. These online components were comparable to using class time to lecture on the content of course materials.

Some of the class time was used for students to work face-to-face on group projects, so this was a natural online extension of that activity. I also wanted to introduce low-stakes quizzing before each Wednesday evening session, to encourage students to open the book and review course material before the discussions.

During the Wednesday discussions, I monitored students' activities and provided feedback on work. There were chapters though that I needed to cover thoroughly in class in the Monday session—the "keepers." These keepers were presented in the face-to-face sessions in the Monday sessions.

Results

According to results from the end-of-course student survey, there was a positive reaction to the online component of the course, such as: pedagogical richness, access to knowledge, social interaction, learner control and ease of course revision. In addition, students appreciated the flexibility of the blended format for getting the work done at more convenient times. Students agreed that more materials were covered in the blended class. They learned more about their classmates than normal because of the online discussions. However, some of the students indicated a preference for a traditional way of learning and offered these reasons: the apparently increased workload, inconvenience of some features in myCourses and time-management difficulties. No students are alike!

Spencer Seung Kim is an associate professor in the manufacturing and mechanical engineering technology/packaging science department in the College of Applied Science and Technology.

Social Sciences

Suzanne Graney
Cultural Diversity in Education
School Psychology Program
College of Liberal Arts
2004–2005 spring quarter

Objectives

Cultural Diversity in Education is a four-credit course, offered in the spring term each year, aimed primarily at second-year school psychology graduate students. Enrollment is open to a limited number of graduate students in programs outside school psychology. I chose to blend this course because:

- I was in the process of choosing a new text for the course and revamping the learning activities

- This course lends itself well to blending, as there is a substantial discussion component

- I plan to blend my Internship I, II, and III courses and participating in the Blended Pilot provided me and my students some experience using the various features of myCourses

Method

I decided to blend 50 percent of the course, meeting with the students two hours per week and requiring an additional two hours for online activities. I then set up the course in two distinct strands: one to be covered through reading and online discussions, the other to be covered through lectures and class activities.

Most of the textbook reading was for the online strand, focused on developing multicultural awareness and learning more specifically about some of the major cultural groups in America. For the first seven weeks, I also had the students read a book on the inequities in public education and how closely those inequities fall along racial lines. They responded once per week to this book in a separate online discussion forum.

In addition to the online discussions, I gave four online quizzes during the quarter. The quizzes covered any material presented during the two weeks immediately prior to the quiz—whether online or in class.

For the in-class strand, I focused on how cultural diversity relates to their future roles as school psychologists. After giving an introduction and overview, I focused on the domains of cross-cultural competence as outlined by the American Psychological Association and adopted by the National Association of School Psychologists. These include, but are not limited to, developing skills in assessment and intervention, working with interpreters and conducting research. Sometimes I assigned additional reading to students to prepare for the in-class strand of the course and I prepared and delivered lectures on these topics as well as in-class discussion or small-group activities.

Results

I think the blended format well in some respects, but I saw some limitations. It cut down on my preparation time, but I spent that time on the back end—reading, and sometimes responding to, the student posts on the online discussion area. I tried to structure questions around each week's topic, but got into a rut after a while asking the same question each week. The students complained that they felt they were running out of things to say.

Some students participated very well in the discussions—posting their own thoughts, reading each other's posts and responding with thoughtful insight. Other students posted the minimum required and I question the degree to which they read their classmates' posts. I tried to encourage more posting above and beyond the minimum by making announcements in class, adding comments to their grade book entries for the week and assigning higher grades to those who went above and beyond the minimum. These tactics worked with some students, but others continued to post their obligatory 200-word initial response and 100-word reply to one classmate. One or two students appeared to have difficulty even posting the minimum set out in the syllabus. I tried to reach these students by offering to help them if they were having trouble, but didn't get a response.

One other issue I had with blended format is that I felt we were missing some of the rich discussion that had occurred in this course during the previous year. This may have occurred anyway, because this particular group of students is quieter as a whole than the group I had taught the year before. But I felt like I wasn't facilitating their learning as much through the online discussions as I may have been able to do in class.

Finally, by separating the course into two strands and doing one in-class and one online, I'm not sure the ideas were as integrated as they should have been.

On the positive side, I did get to hear from students online who rarely speak up in class. I felt I had a better handle on what each student was thinking, because of their posts on the discussion board. I do think some students opened up more online than they would have in class.

Conclusion

Overall, I'd say the blending of this course was successful, but I would probably change some things if I decide to blend it again next year. I might limit the online portion of the class, saving more time to discuss the textbook in the face-to-face format. Or I might try to build in more crossover between online and face-to-face activities, so the course feels more integrated, rather than separated into two distinct strands, one online and the other face-to-face.

Postscript

I have continued to teach Cultural Diversity in Education in a blended format. However, I cut back on the online portion so it is 25 percent blended. Over the years I also cut back on the amount of posting required. During the spring of 2006, I removed the textbook portion from the online discussions and moved it to the classroom instead. That left two strands for the discussion board—weekly reflections and discussion of the Kozol book.

In class we discussed domains of cultural competence and characteristics of various cultural groups. I also dropped the quizzes. The 2006 class commented on their evaluations that the online posting was too much, so in 2007 I reduced the online requirements further by alternating weeks between check-ins and Kozol readings. Although I still get comments about the online requirements being burdensome, I feel this is a reasonable amount of work for students and will not reduce it further.

Every year, I entertain the idea of abolishing the online portion of the class and making it completely face-to-face. This year I told the students at the beginning of the quarter that I would be willing to change the format during the quarter if they believed it would be beneficial for them to have in-class rather than online discussions. They did not make such a request, and I did get positive comments about the online portion. I have learned that most students embrace the online interactions, but a few in each group do not enjoy it and would prefer strictly face-to-face instruction. Unfortunately with the way our program is structured, we are not able to offer students a choice of format, as one section of each course is typically offered and all students are required to take it.

Suzanne Graney is an assistant professor in the school psychology department in the College of Liberal Arts.

Paul DeCotis
Energy Policy: Special Topics
Public Policy Department
College of Liberal Arts
2004-2005 spring quarter

Objectives

Energy Policy: Special Topics provides an overview of energy resources, technologies, global needs and policies designed to ensure clean and sustainable supplies of reasonably priced energy for the future. The course deliberately focuses on the factors that influence energy production and use, technology development and energy resource allocation; with particular emphasis on the role that public policy plays in national as well as global energy markets and economies. The development of U.S. energy policy was of particular concern, as the U.S. Congress and President were in the process of drafting comprehensive energy legislation during the term of the 2004-2005 course.

Upon completion of the course, students are expected to have a firm understanding of various energy technologies, their impacts on society and the policy mechanisms that affect their use. Students are also expected to gain insights and develop skills for identifying relevant energy and related policy issues, conduct policy analysis and develop policy alternatives and understand various stakeholder interests and how they influence policymaking. In summary, students are expected to demonstrate competency in their abilities to:

- Identify relevant energy and related public policy issues

- Conduct policy analysis using various analytical methods, including life cycle benefit-cost analyses

- Assess the near- and longer-term qualitative implications of selected energy and related public policies

- Formulate strategies necessary to successfully enact energy policies

Method

I chose to offer Energy Policy as a blended course meeting three times in the traditional classroom setting, with the remaining sessions and activities conducted online. The class met the first night of the term, mid-term and the last week of classes.

The course was taught in three modules, each focusing on a different aspect of the subject matter. All activities in the learning module were coordinated—including readings, class discussions and break-outs, online discussions and written assignments. Classroom activities included lecture and discussion; small group breakouts with reporting out; debates among students on energy technologies; energy, economic, and environmental policies and their interactions; and the roles of government, industry and consumers in energy markets. The mid-term class included a student role play—for example, students testifying before Congress, arguing for budget increases before the U.S. Department of Energy or developing and debating energy policy from various stakeholder perspectives. One text book and three to four energy policy related reports provided the reading foundation for the course.

The course had both undergraduate and graduate students, with the majority being graduate students. While all assignments are the same regardless of student status, significantly more effort and performance was expected of graduate students—including more in-depth understanding of issues and relevant concepts, more frequent participation in discussions (in class and online), greater thoughtfulness in their participation and leadership in activities.

Students are expected to complete three papers submitted and graded online and one final group project of choice—requiring instructor approval. Regular participation in online discussions was required and monitored two to three times weekly. E-mail communication occurred at least twice weekly with the instructor providing guidance and direction to students and offering feedback to the class as necessary on activities to date. Personal e-mail correspondence was common—often imitated by students themselves.

Results

The course progressed well and mostly as expected during the quarter. Student participation and leadership in discussions was a bit uneven, but not unexpected. Self-motivated students participated more through myCourses and initiated more online discussion threads than students who were less self-motivated or generally uncomfortable with the blended course format. In addition, through the three student papers and online discussions, it was evident that not all students were devoting the time necessary to read and comprehend the reading materials required for this course. These observations, however, are not unique to blended courses, as student performance is often uneven in a traditional classroom setting. A student's desire to learn and perform to expectation proved again to be the greater driving influence on student achievement.

Students for the most part were engaged, with very few exceptions. The group project proved very worthwhile in conveying competencies in the subject matter and the student group activities proved challenging yet exciting. Overall, the course progressed as expected and student feedback throughout the course was regular and helpful to me in monitoring learning activities and making minor adjustments to the course along the way.

> *"Every effort needs to be made to keep students engaged online–this means offering websites and other electronic materials and references to read and communicating freely and often with students, both as a group and individually."*

The blended course format met most of my own expectations, with a few exceptions, as discussed below. First, some observations:

- Participation of students in discussion boards was uneven in both frequency and thoughtfulness of content. Clearly, just as a classroom setting would reveal, some students participated more than others and with different degrees of intensity

- Graduate students, for the most part, accepted the challenge to meet higher expectations and went well beyond undergraduate students in their activities—accepting challenges to do additional work and research and share their work and findings with other students

- myCourses software is easy to use and provides a useful platform for blended or fully online learning

Modifications

While the course went well generally, I have found that every effort needs to be made to keep students engaged online—this means offering websites and other electronic materials and references to read and communicating freely and often with students, both as a group and individually. In addition, it is important to identify student strengths and developmental needs through their writings and communications with limited personal contact—this requires taking time to read and respond to student assignments and pushing students to attain higher levels of achievement—and only through their meeting or falling short of these expectations can the instructor understand a students unique abilities and needs.

For the next course offering in the blended format, I recommend the following:

- Students enrolled in a blended learning course are made more aware of the online learning environment, including its similarities and differences to traditional classroom learning. Perhaps some introductory training might help

- Prior to the start of the quarter (or as early as possible), instructors should introduce students to the course via e-mail and provide an overview of the blended course format and expectations

- More credit (higher grading weight) is given to online learning activities, to encourage greater and more even student participation in online discussions and assignments

Conclusion

In conclusion, I must commend RIT and the Online Learning department for the innovativeness of the blended course pilot. I received a great deal of support from Online Learning and appreciated the opportunity to be a part of the Blended Pilot.

Postscript

After teaching Energy Policy as a blended course three times now, many earlier findings are reinforced and several suggestions are offered to generally apply to blended course offerings. Blended courses can be as effective in facilitating and reinforcing student leaning as classroom teaching provided that:

- Students are able and willing to accept a less formally structured regime of learning

- Students demonstrate responsibility in pursuit of their own learning

- Instructors are able to find the right formula given the student body (unique to each course offering) that entices them and excites them about learning

As I refined the course with each successive offering, more time and a greater proportion of the students grade was assigned to online discussion and electronic activities. Separate online discussion boards were established for each team of students so that they could coordinate and share documents and dialogue between classes and throughout the quarter. This proved particularly helpful when students were working on projects together or planning their role playing exercise.

Having more than 23 years of teaching experience—including classroom teaching, mail correspondence, fully online and blended teaching, for several different colleges and universities at the graduate level, undergraduate and mixed grades—I put in approximately an equal number of hours regardless of format. The types of activities differ and the times of the day devoted to the course differ, with 24-hour per day flexibility for planning and participating and leading student learning using the electronic format. After years of teaching and in various formats, I value the unique learning opportunity and flexibility provided to students and instructors in the blended format.

> "It is important to identify student strengths and developmental needs through their writings and communications—and push students to attain higher levels of achievement. Only through their meeting or falling short of these expectations can the instructor understand a student's unique abilities and needs."

As advice to colleges and universities interested in blended learning, I suggest that students be screened for their readiness to accept the responsibilities for blended learning; students be at or about the same level of educational experience and competence in the subject matter generally (for instance, allowing first-term freshman to take a course with doctoral students provides challenges both for the instructor and students); and that students be deliberately apprised of the differences between traditional classroom and online learning environments.

Paul DeCotis is an adjunct professor in the public policy department in the College of Liberal Arts and the deputy secretary for energy for New York State.

Judy Porter

Fear of Crime & Corrections
Criminal Justice Department
College of Liberal Arts
2004-2005 winter quarter

Background

I had two courses I taught this quarter that were part of the Blended Pilot. I had not taught a blended course prior to this quarter, though I had used some of the myCourses options last quarter and found them to be helpful.

Method

I used an online syllabus, facilitated online discussions, had a virtual office, sent messages, used the grade book and posted lectures and other materials in the content section. Students were encouraged to use all of these features and seemed to enjoy using them once they had learned the necessary skills. Some of them were more proficient than others.

I used the announcements or news section quite a bit to update students on any changes in the course, or problems, and to let them know where certain items were posted—such as exam questions, reminders of due dates and paper requirements. I found this feature to be very helpful.

The gradebook was a great feature and allowed me to keep track of student's progress and easily figure out their grades using the weighted feature.

The content and the discussions feature allowed me to post both individual and group work assignments and extra readings that pertained to the subjects we were exploring. This allowed us to keep up to date on current events, as well.

I was called away one week on a family emergency and was able, via the Internet, to continue with class which was a great help. The students were able to continue with the readings and post their work online and receive feedback from me about their responses.

Results

I did encounter initial resistance to the blended course format, as some of the students reflected they had experienced some difficulties with such classes prior to taking this class and indeed some of them said they would not have taken this class had they known in advance it was blended.

However, I promised to continue to address their concerns throughout the course, explained we were a pilot project and that I was interested in learning how to use this format effectively. We discussed the use of myCourses throughout the quarter in the classroom, which led to some problems and complaints early on about using too much class time to work on the blended project. But as we learned what was working for us and what was not, we used less in-class time to work out the kinks.

> *"I did find that, at times, I was frustrated with lack of in-class time and had to work on paring down lectures and films. At other times, I was grateful for the break from in-class time and the ability to work with students online."*

In attempting to address some of the problems last quarter concerning the last-minute cramming of material prior to an exam—students had told me they did this and that was why in-class discussions were not going well—I had them post summaries of the assigned readings each week to the online discussion area, and then post online reactions to the readings. This seemed to work well, as the discussions both in class and online seemed to be well informed. However, students complained of workload, so at the middle of the quarter I excused them from the summary postings but not the discussion postings. It seems that the number of discussion postings went down and I would say the learning also suffered. So I believe I will require the summaries again next quarter.

I took the opportunity to post a number of articles and websites that appeared to have relevance to course discussions. It was informative for me to see where the online discussions went and what piece of knowledge seemed to be missing. That gave me the ability to address these concerns both in class and online.

The students liked the discussions, hated the summaries, liked the lectures posted, and did not use the virtual office very much as they usually just e-mailed me directly with their questions. I had assigned 20 percent of their grade to in-class and online participation.

I liked seeing where their thoughts were, filling in the gaps, posting updates, using the grade book, having the ability to send messages both to the entire class and to selected individuals, and the file section to post extras that I hoped they would use.

I was frustrated in the beginning with my lack of expertise, and the students' lack of expertise as well, in using myCourses. Perhaps next time I will have someone from Online Learning come to my class to help us with the technology. I did not avail myself as much as I would have liked of the proffered help from the Online Learning staff. This was a factor of time constraints on my part. I did enjoy the luncheon and presentation I attended and found that helpful.

I did find that, at times, I was frustrated with lack of in-class time and had to work on paring down lectures and films. At other times, I was grateful for the break from in-class time and the ability to work with students online. This depended on my own time needs and the difficulty of the readings. I believe I heard that I could make films or snippets of films available online, which is an option I will explore for next quarter.

I tried putting students in charge of posting questions for discussion and had some success with this. When I responded, I think I had a tendency to overwhelm the students and perhaps put a damper on their discussions, so I kept my part in the online discussions to a minimum and this seemed to help. I would post announcements that addressed the concern I had about the online discussion or address in lecture during class time what I believed needed to be brought forward. I also feel that the increased interaction with students helped them to feel more comfortable in class and with consulting me outside of class.

Conclusion

All in all, I found the blended class to be a benefit to both students and myself and plan on continuing to use blended classes in future and build my skills in this area.

I am grateful for the opportunity to participate in the Blended Pilot. I learned a great deal about my students and their knowledge base. This enabled me to address issues and concerns about misinformation or lack of information both in class and online.

Postscript

I have been teaching all of my courses as blended learning. Some of them have a minimal amount of time online while others have as much as 50 percent of the class time online.

A consistent component of my online coursework is the use of the discussion section. I have had students tell me that this keeps their minds on the subject at hand and helps them to learn more about the topic from their fellow students as well as the in-class work and their text books. Online discussion allows me, the instructor, to gauge the knowledge of the students and to provide further readings and assistance to help them in gaining the required knowledge, as well as allowing me to provide thought provoking readings and links to enhance their learning experience. Often they provide the links and readings for each other and enhance my knowledge!

> *"The gradebook is like having a personal assistant—I don't know what I would do without it. It lets me keep up-to-date and gives students the opportunity to have all their grades in one place to keep track of their progress."*

Students who may have a more difficult time in the classroom letting their voices be heard are on equal grounds in the discussion section—I learn much more about my deaf and hard-of-hearing students, students for whom English is a second language, and shy students in the online discussion area than in the classroom. As we interact with each other, we become more cohesive as a learning group. The give-and-take process generally works very well and most students express an appreciation of this opportunity. The discussion section also opens up in-class discussion as we can expand on our thoughts.

The dropbox is very important to me as it allows my students to submit their work in a timely manner that is convenient for them. It also allows me to provide feedback to them quickly and conveniently without having to bring them in to the office or wait until class time. Additionally, subjects that are somewhat sensitive, such as topics in the seminar in sexual violence or the minority groups and the criminal justice system classes, can be dealt with in a confidential manner by having students submit their work in the dropbox. In this way, they are assured no one else is going to see their thoughts and experiences unless they choose to discuss them openly online or in the classroom. This is very helpful as students explore their own experiences, feelings and thoughts on controversial topics or very personal topics.

The means to provide an announcement or news section and to send out class e-mails to alert students of changes has been very helpful to me. The availability of a "virtual office space" (a question and answer topic in the discussions area) has allowed the students to contact me quickly and allows me to respond just as quickly to questions and concerns. When I have created a question and answer area, students will often help each other with mundane class questions such as where to access a lecture or a due date.

The content section is wonderful not only for the convenience for students to have access to the syllabus, the lectures and readings, but it allows me to post extra readings on topics that may interest students but we do not have enough time to cover completely in the class room.

Of course, the gradebook is like having a personal assistant—I don't know what I would do without it. It lets me keep up-to-date and gives students the opportunity to have all their grades in one place to keep track of their progress.

Judy Porter is a professor in the criminal justice department in the College of Liberal Arts.

Kijana Crawford
Foundations of Sociology
Department of Sociology and Anthropology
College of Liberal Arts
2004-2005 winter quarter

Objectives

In blending my Foundations of Sociology course, one of the objectives was to introduce students to the basic concepts in sociology, fundamental approaches, theories and methods through group processes. Another objective was to increase critical interaction between students through written work, research and developing leadership skills.

Method

Initially six groups were created along with 10 group projects. Equal points were assigned to both individual and group participation. Students were also given guidelines and expectations in group processes. The first week was spent in a traditional face-to-face setting. Classes met on Wednesday morning from 8-9:50 a.m. This time was spent lecturing and responding to questions previously raised on the online discussion area. Students were also given an opportunity to do two individual assignments and to take two exams online.

Results

Although I created an assignment that allowed students to do several exercises to become familiar with myCourses, it became clear that the level of computer literacy ranged from never being exposed to myCourses to being very comfortable with it. Students who were computer literate quickly became frustrated with those who were not.

On a positive note, I was able to observe group dynamics online. Through the discussions, I was able to determine the level and frequency of each student's contribution to the papers, who took on leadership roles and who never contributed. Often students confronted each other about their lack of participation.

Students often expressed frustration with the quality of their team members' writing and lack of motivation. One student discovered that a member of his team plagiarized his contribution to the paper. Members of the group confronted him in the group and chose not to submit his work.

One student asked to be assigned to another group. Although she was not assigned to another group, we did discuss the value of working in groups and how you deal with problems you may encounter.

Towards the middle of the quarter, most of the students were academically at the level where I wanted them to be. Those who were not were the same students who lacked motivation and computer skills at the beginning of the course. At the end of the course, all students were academically at the level where I wanted them to be with the exception of one.

Modifications

- Implement a system where students can fire each other from teams and specify the process and circumstances
- Design an equal number of group and individual activities

Conclusion

I was too ambitious in designing this course. There were too many students in the course and I designed too many exercises. Since I was able to and did read the discussions in the groups, I did not take into consideration the large amount of time required to read and grade the group posts.

Overall, the experience was worthwhile and I will do it again.

Postscript

I am still teaching Foundations of Sociology as a blended course.

I have noticed the increased computer literacy of the students who enroll in the course and, in particular, the improved ability of students to navigate myCourses. [Ed's note: myCourses was upgraded to a new system, Desire2Learn, in the summer of 2005.] This has alleviated a lot of student frustration as well as allowed more time to be spent on course content.

Through my initial observations of student group dynamics online, I was able to tailor certain aspects of the course in a way that increased total student participation and enhanced individual student success and learning.

I cut down on the number of exercises and I began to focus more on group discussion and incorporating more individual assignments into the course. In an effort to get students to take on leadership roles and stimulate motivation and participation, I presented fairly open-ended discussion topics and assignments to groups and only instructed them to work together to solve problems as opposed to providing strict instructional guidance.

The individual assignments were designed to reinforce many of the concepts brought up in the group assignments as well as those that were not explored to my satisfaction.

"Students reflected on and analyzed their experiences and issues that arose in their groups. This approach enabled the medium of instruction to become an invaluable sociological-pedagogical tool."

Face-to-face lecture time was utilized for the purposes of clarification and elaboration. It was also used as a platform for students to air group and individual grievances.

Throughout the process, students reflected on and analyzed their experiences and issues that arose in their groups. This approach enabled the medium of instruction to become an invaluable sociological-pedagogical tool and allowed group conflict to add merit and insight to the concepts as opposed to being an impediment to the learning process.

Kijana Crawford is an associate professor in the sociology and anthropology department in the College of Liberal Arts.

Peter Hauser

History and Systems of Psychology
Department of Psychology
College of Liberal Arts
2005-2006 winter quarter

Background

The History and Systems of Psychology course provides background to the development of current psychological perspectives. It examines beliefs, practices, achievements and limitations of various systems of psychology from Greek times through to the late 20th century.

Objectives

Upon completion of this course, students will:

- Be able to describe how the field of psychology developed and evolved

- Be able to identify individuals who have made major contributions

- Be able to describe the various systems of psychology

- Develop better presentation skills

- Develop online discussion skills

Method

Traditionally, History and Systems of Psychology has been a lecture course where most of the in-class time is spent listening to lectures offered by the instructor and being tested on lectures and assigned readings. Students have been required to write a term paper about a psychologist who has made a major contribution to the field or on a specific system within psychology. Some instructors have required students to give an in-class presentation on their paper at the end of the quarter. The major problem with this instruction method is that it is boring. It is a challenge to maintain the students' attention and interest in the topic. Students often fall behind assigned readings and this always has a negative impact on the depth and breath of the in-class discussions.

Lectures

My blended version of History and Systems of Psychology involved 50 percent in-class lectures and 50 percent online discussions and quizzes. The reduction of in-class time was compensated for by more assigned readings. The assigned readings covered the various systems of psychology, while the in-class lectures focused more on the contributions of the field of philosophy to the development of psychology and early history of psychology.

Weekly quizzes

Students were assigned weekly online quizzes that consisted of 30 multiple-choice questions that were based on the chapters they were assigned to read. For each quiz, approximately 50 questions were uploaded into the myCourses quiz question library, and 30 random questions were automatically chosen for each student. The multiple-choice answers were also randomized to prevent students from sharing the answers for specific questions. The students' scores on the quizzes were automatically uploaded to the myCourses gradebook and the correct answers were provided at the end of the quiz period.

Weekly online team discussions

Early in the quarter I created teams of three to four students and appointed team leaders. Each team was assigned a set of five essay questions wherein each student had to choose one essay question to answer and respond to at least two of the other students' answers. Each team was given the same set of five questions each week. The team discussions were restricted—students were not able to read other teams' answers. The team leader was responsible for keeping track of the team members' progress and the teams were graded as a whole, based on their participation. I monitored the discussions to ensure the quality of the responses were appropriate. With quality standardized by the instructor across groups, it made it possible to fairly grade on participation alone. Team members had the right to make a recommendation to the instructor to have a team member voted off the team and graded individually. The team leader and I provided team members who were falling behind with ample opportunity to catch up before the team felt a need to vote off a member.

Team presentations

Each team was also assigned to give a 20-minute in-class presentation at the end of the quarter on a topic that has been discussed throughout the history of psychology (i.e., views on psychopathology and types of treatment recommended, mind-body relationships or nature versus nurture). The presentations were to include the past history, current practice and thought and future directions on the chosen topic. Students presented fragments of their final presentation in class throughout the quarter and were evaluated by their peers as well as the instructor (using an evaluation form with a Likert scale). The teams were ranked based on the results of the evaluations and a specific grade was assigned to each rank. The final presentation was evaluated in a similar manner, but by guest judges (students, faculty, and administrators) rather than by peers. Students were assigned to work on their presentations on a weekly basis via an online discussion forum in myCourses that was restricted to the team members only. Similarly, team members could recommend a member to be voted out of the team and graded individually based on a deficit in the quality or quantity of their participation.

Results

Lectures

The reduction in the students' seat time in-class resulted in a reduction in lectures offered in class (a 50 percent reduction). Nevertheless, more material was covered than previously in a non-blended session because of the online features offered in this course as discussed in the following subsections.

Weekly quizzes

The preparation for the weekly quizzes was the most time-consuming component of this blended course for me. I had to use a software program in the Online Learning department to convert the questions to HTML format then had to follow more than 25 steps to get the quizzes uploaded onto myCourses, set up the randomization feature and connect them to the gradebook. This process took over an hour the first time I tried to do it but, by the end of the quarter, I was able to achieve this task in less than 10 minutes. The students reported that the weekly quizzes took them between one- to two-hours to complete. Even though this was an open-book quiz, not all of the students obtained a perfect score on this quiz. The class average was 86 percent correct.

Weekly online team discussions

The weekly team discussions were more successful than I initially anticipated when I developed this course. The breath and depth of the topics the students discussed exceeded my expectations. Each student successfully answered one assigned essay question as expected, but responded to more of the other students' essay answers than required, and some of the discussions continued beyond the allocated time for the assigned chapter discussion. Students asked each other questions and related topics to experiences in their lives and to other materials they learned in this and other courses. The average number of posts per team made by the end of the quarter was 178 posts (approximately 45 posts per student). I participated in the team discussions when students had questions (in their responses to student essays) that could not be answered by the other team members, when the quality of a students' essay needed work and when I had something to add to the discussion.

"The use of asynchronous online discussions removed the barriers that often exist for out-of-classroom work between deaf/hard-of-hearing students and hearing students."

Team presentations

Teams began working on their presentations at the beginning of the quarter within a discussion forum that was developed for each team for this assignment. The average number of online posts made by each team was 285 (approximately 75 posts per student). The students discussed and voted on the topics they wanted to cover in their presentations and shared outlines, drafts PowerPoint slides and scripts. This enabled teams to work together throughout the week and throughout the quarter even when they were not in class or meeting with each other in person. I followed the students' progress by reading their online discussions and I was able to provide immediate feedback and advice.

Other online features

In the beginning of the course, students were asked to introduce themselves online in a specific discussion forum that was developed for this purpose. Although there were only 15 students in this class, 119 posts were made. This enabled the students to get to know each other better than students in a non-blended course, because this type of discussion rarely occurs within the classroom, especially among all members of the class. Students began talking to each other within this discussion forum, sharing their mutual interests in specific hobbies or life experiences. I believe that this enabled the class to build relationships that were positively reflected within the classroom when they had in-class discussions. The students affect on and interest in each other was substantially different than I have experienced in my non-blended courses.

Another discussion forum was created for any course-related questions or comments. This forum had a total of 126 posts by the end of the quarter. This reduced my need to respond to individual e-mails about course content and assignments. In my non-blended courses, I often find myself having to answer the same question to several students via e-mail. This also helped students who might have had the same question but did not intend to actually ask the question or students who have not thought of the question but benefited from the answer.

The development and maintenance of a new blended course takes substantially more time than a traditional in-class course. This is because the instructor has to create the appropriate tools (i.e., quizzes, discussions and uploading of lectures) within myCourses. However, once everything has been created, it can easily be imported to future sessions of the course. The maintenance of a live blended course is still time-consuming. The instructor needs to check the course discussions on a regular basis. The total amount of time an instructor spends on reading and posting messages in any given week can go beyond the amount of time it would have taken to give an additional lecture that week. A total of 2,095 messages were posted in this course.

I found it necessary to check messages on a regular basis (i.e., every day, during the day and evenings, including weekends), which made it much more manageable than if I attempted to read messages and post responses only once or twice a week. If I did the latter, it would cause two problems: (1) it would require me to allocate a significant time period to achieve this task in one sitting; and (2) students would not feel as motivated to participate in online discussions if I had not provided immediate responses.

Even though the amount of time I spent throughout the week, day and night, was significant, I was always motivated to catch up on the recent online discussions, as were my students because the discussions were lively. I believe this had a positive impact on my and my students' interest and intrinsic motivation in being committed to this course.

The inclusion of weekly online quizzes and team discussions allowed the students to learn more material than what was provided in the course lectures. When providing a lecture, it is often difficult to tell where students had trouble understanding the theories and principles discussed. The weekly discussion forum and the results of the weekly quizzes enabled me to see where students were having difficulty and to provide additional instruction by posting relevant messages online. Within the team presentations discussion forums, the students applied what they learned from the chapters (via quizzes and essay assignments) to their projects, which further helped them with their learning of the course material.

This course had six deaf/hard-of-hearing students in addition to nine hearing students. Three of the four team leaders were deaf/hard-of-hearing. I intentionally appointed deaf/hard-of-hearing team leaders for several reasons:

1. They often do not have an opportunity to be a group leader in a mainstream classroom

2. They typically have extensive experience using online means for everyday communicating

3. They usually are better at controlling the pace of in-person discussions to ensure all members are included—when discussions are managed by non-deaf individuals, the leaders often do not pause to wait for interpreters to finish interpreting so everyone has an equal chance to participate

The use of asynchronous online discussions removed the barriers that often exist for out-of-classroom work between deaf/hard-of-hearing students and hearing students because it is difficult to obtain interpreting services for these in-person meetings. Additionally, this enabled the hearing and the deaf/hard-of-hearing students to get to know each other and learn how to work with each other. At the end of the quarter, both groups of students reported that they learned a lot from each other and enjoyed having an opportunity to work together. They also reported that this type of interaction rarely occurred in their other classes.

Conclusion

I strongly believe that blending courses enhances learning. Based on the results of blending the History and Systems of Psychology course, compared to the students in my previous non-blended session of this course, the blended students learned more material, participated more in discussions (both online and in-class) and were more able to integrate and apply what they learned. The use of online discussions also enabled students to get to know each other better and for deaf/hard-of-hearing and hearing students to work together without communication barriers. I believe I could significantly improve my teaching and my students' learning if I blended all of my courses or at least used more of the myCourses features in all of my courses.

Peter Hauser is an assistant professor in the research and teacher education studies department in the National Technical Institute for the Deaf at RIT.

Peter Manzi

Introduction to Psychology
Department of Psychology
College of Liberal Arts
2004-2005 fall quarter

Objectives

In blending the Introduction to Psychology course, one of the objectives was to get students to respond to questions on a discussion board. This required that they write for purposes other than strictly for the evaluation of writing skills. I provided guidelines for how to respond on the board, something one cannot do in a regular classroom—that is, one cannot tell a student after they have voiced an opinion that their form or content was weak. Online, I was able to give written feedback on their posts.

Another objective of blending the course was to increase interaction between students. In effect, reducing face-to-face time would represent an increase in discussion board and e-mail interaction among students, although the level of e-mail interaction was private and not trackable. I had noticed that traditional PSY 101 classes did not have much meaningful interaction among students. I could have required each student to print out a log of e-mail interaction among group members—an empirical approach that might encourage, if not enforce, this student-to-student e-mail activity—but I decided to be less formal and did not do that.

Method

I equally divided my course into online and classroom components.

Since half of the course was to be done online—in a user friendly text-based environment—students were required to participate both in class and outside of class. I offered an online discussion forum where students could ask questions about assignments, readings, etc., so they were not limited to asking in class only. This, to me, was a great advantage—having asynchronous or anytime discussions and interactive feedback.

The class was offered at night and, instead of running from 6 to 10 p.m.—when most students are tired, lethargic or unenthusiastic after a full day of activity—the class ended at 9 p.m. Also, 30 minutes of class time was used for working on a small group project.

I created a project selection area in myCourses where students could identify each other and project topics. Students were encouraged to form an e-mail group for members of their project group. I could have set up small discussion groups in myCourses, based on training I received from Online Learning, but I wanted the students to take responsibility for doing this and use their own instincts for forming groups as some may know each other from other settings. The instructor can not do everything for them and then expect students to be independent and responsible for the group process and their performance.

"The students responded really well to this method of instruction. Since I had taught the same course with the same materials the previous year, I had a good opportunity for comparison."

We spent the first two weeks of the course in a traditional face-to-face setting. During that time, we did some practice myCourses exercises to establish familiarity with the technology and platform methods, where to find exams, how to post, and how to send attachments. Most students were familiar with myCourses or expressed no concerns about it. Two students had to get an RIT e-mail account, which delayed them a bit in the first two weeks. (I had announced this need the first week of classes.)

From the third week onwards, we met once a week in the classroom and had an online activity (a choice of three discussion questions, based on the readings for that week) for the next six weeks.

I queried students about the use of a chat room, akin to office hours, and most said they probably would not use it.

The discussion questions assignment was required and graded. Only if a response was poor did I notify students by e-mail, and not on the board, out of respect. This only happened a few times in a class of 32 students. I used open-ended questions when responding to their entries on the discussion board or made "food for thought" statements that added to the book's material. I offered concise praise and support on most discussion postings. I found students were concerned when I did not respond to their entries.

Students were encouraged to respond to each others' postings, but that rarely happened in the beginning. When I mentioned this in class, they said there was little point since these were no-opinion questions. I think some students were self-conscious about being candid with other students. I explained that responses were educational experiences done in an informal format. The participation improved somewhat, although several students habitually posted late, which resulted in a deduction in points for attendance and participation. I sent reminders out via e-mail broadcast asking non-posters to post or pay the piper. One can't do this type of notification in a one-night-a-week classroom setting nearly as effectively.

Exams

A take-home exam consisting of multiple-choice, open-ended questions and short essays was posted on a Thursday and due on a Sunday—giving students ample time to complete the exam. Students sent their exams through the myCourses dropbox or mostly via e-mail, perhaps a sign that the path of least resistance was used. No students said they had any questions about the exams (three exams, each covering 4-5 chapters), which is so rare when giving in-class exams. This freed up time—rather than spending a total of nine hours taking three exams in class, students did them at home. I asked them how long the exams took and they said three to four-and-a-half hours.

Lectures

I posted a three- to four-page summary with notes for each book chapter in the content section, in addition to covering material in-class. This was well liked by students—they said the book was technical, the hands-on in-class activities were good, and the lectures pulled it all together. I played videos, cassettes and did experiments with the students in addition to a peripatetic style of lecturing and walking up to students to ask them questions. This was a stadium-seating lecture-type classroom and students were spread out across a large area.

Group project

The week of finals, Week 11, was used for a small-group multi-media presentation. Students were also required to post a one-page summary of the project on an online discussion board for the whole class to read. Were it not for a final exam the same week, I would have asked students to respond with at least two postings to each of the eight group presentations. One of the problems with using the discussions board with 32 students is the sheer volume of postings. I recommend that a blended introductory course be restricted to 22 students.

Results

The students responded really well to this method of instruction. Since I had taught the same course with the same materials the previous year, I had a good opportunity for comparison. Part of what I wanted to accomplish was not to lose some of the impetus of the full-time, face-to-face model, while creating more opportunities for writing and student interaction. This was successful in that students discussed readings about 30 percent more than they would have in a regular classroom setting.

In these online discussions, I did not grade for grammar or language accuracy. The point of the exercise was for developing effective communication and the written expression of reading content and lecture materials. In accord with Writing Across the Curriculum protocols that emphasize low-stakes writing, students were encouraged to exchange ideas freely without being penalized for language errors. Final grades in this course as compared with my previous traditional course at this time in the quarter were about the same, perhaps a 10-20 percent increase in the number of As and Bs. When students were failing, it was due to, (a) not completing assignments or being very tardy with them, (b) being very poorly prepared (not reading all of the assignments or doing them at the last minute) or, (c) personal, family or health reasons (I am always amazed a the coincidence of deaths or car accidents in the family and rapid-onset illnesses during the last two weeks of a quarter!).

Peter Manzi is an adjunct professor in the psychology department in the College of Liberal Arts.

Jennifer Lukomski
School Psychology Practicum
School Psychology Department
College of Liberal Arts
2005-2006 fall quarter

Background

Our school psychology program at RIT is unique in that our full-time students are placed in a school practicum setting for one day a week when they start taking classes in our Educational Specialist level program. This practicum experience provides them with the opportunity to experience three different school or child/adolescent mental health settings totaling approximately 360 hours prior to their third year of training—their internship year. This practicum sequence course consists of participating one six-hour day in the field each week, with supervision by a field placement supervisor, and attending a weekly two-hour seminar class facilitated by the university based practicum supervisor.

Objective

With excitement and apprehension, I approached using a blended learning format that combines classroom instruction with online learning for the school psychology practicum course.

My primary objective was to explore how online learning could supplement in-class seminar discussions. I believed that for students who are quiet and students who are deaf or hard-of-hearing, online interactions would level the playing ground with regards to accessibility.

A more lofty long term vision for introducing the online component in the practicum class was the possibility that exposure and use of this online supervision format during training may translate into a community of school psychologists who adopt online peer supervision once they are school psychology practitioners.

I welcomed the experience, yet was confronted with anxiety about my lack of knowledge and expertise in online learning and using the technology. Over the summer, I eased my way into the process and started to learn about navigating myCourses with consultation and support from Online Learning. I learned how to set up the content section, news items and discussions (forums and topics). I attended a luncheon on blended learning and continued to modify the course based on feedback from students and from interfacing with the technology and the online learning process.

Method

In the fall quarter, two sections totaling 20 students met during orientation week to discuss the practicum course requirements. One of their first assignments was to become familiar with myCourses by introducing themselves online. Following four weeks of meeting face-to-face in the respective sections (10 students per section), we then met online for four weeks. For the last two classes (including exam week) we met face-to-face. Since all the news items and course contents applied to both sections, the two course sections were merged into one myCourses shell, meaning all students entered the same site. The breakout for the two sections occurred in the weekly asynchronous discussion forums, with each section having its own designated (but not private) topic area to post reflections. The students had the option to check out what the students in the other section were doing, however, they were only required to read and respond to the reflections of the students in their section.

Students wrote reflection papers and submitted them on a weekly basis. In the traditional model, the reflection paper was handed to the instructor and discussed in class. In the blended model, the reflection paper was posted for the class to read and respond to. The reflection paper was not a reiteration of what they did that day. Rather it was an opportunity for the students to highlight one activity or event that they observed or participated in during their practicum day.

Students posted their reflections online by Wednesday afternoon. The class had time to comment on postings until Friday. I followed the discussion. On Friday or Saturday I summarized, answered items that needed clarification and posed questions on what was brought up.

Figuring out how I was to facilitate the online interaction was the challenge. Since this is not a didactic course, but a supervision course, I pondered on how to best provide the supervision and allow for students to freely interact—providing me with information on their background knowledge (whether accurate or not) and their thinking processes. I did not want to step in too quickly with my comments, experiences, answers and questions. Instead of responding individually to each student's reflection, I summarized the themes for the week and pointed out gaps and inconsistencies by posing questions. I individualized my summary comments for each group by mentioning names of students in my summary.

Results

At the end of the quarter I asked the students to fill out an evaluation form.

Students' responses to the general question of, "What was the online learning experience like for you?" were primarily positive. Many students felt that both the breadth and depth of learning about each others' experience was enhanced. Students wrote:

> I liked the online experience overall. I thought I got to know more about each person's site and experiences than I may have with the in-class format.

> It was enjoyable. I think I participated more than I would in a classroom setting. I really like the online format rather than sitting in a group of students I don't know very well. I didn't feel shy about sharing my input or asking questions from others. It was easier to share and I didn't feel I would be as judged as a person.

> I enjoyed the online learning experience because it really opened up the discussion and we got to know our classmates better.

> I liked the online class. It actually caused me to spend more time on the class and I liked how I could refer back to entries.

One student summed up the experience for her by commenting on the use of the technology. She reported:

> It was definitely confusing at first. I had never had an online course and was unsure of how to navigate the site or what was even on the site. Once I was used to the format it was very easy to use.

Regarding the ease of using myCourses, every student submitted and responded to others reflections. Based on the participation online, I assumed that all the students were aware of the other sections of myCourses.

Even though I made a few announcements in class regarding the various areas to explore on myCourses, to my dismay, towards the end of the course a few students informed me that they did not realize that throughout the quarter I was posting news items related to my site visits, as well as course modifications (even though I would send them e-mail messages to go to the news section to read the items posted.)

Additionally, a few students did not realize that they had access to the course materials (log sheets, evaluation forms, practicum plan and syllabus) under the content section. Furthermore, some students, who on a weekly basis posted their reflections in the discussion area, were unaware about the other discussion areas located on that same page.

Overall these graduate students' cognitive levels are above average and they are motivated to learn so the reasoning for why they did not explore or figure out that the existence of these various sections on myCourses may be due more to a lack of experience and lack of comfort with using technology. One student did comment that she felt the home page was too crowded with other information.

A student said, "I think I participated more than I would in a classroom setting. I didn't feel shy about sharing my input or asking questions from others. It was easier to share and I didn't feel I would be as judged as a person."

A few students' comments on the overall online experience compared and contrasted the online format to the face-to-face format. Comments included:

I think I got more details from the online posts, but better discussions in the classroom.

Interesting to hear experiences, but difficult to engage in a conversation.

I liked reading everyone's reflections, but I think it's more personal to meet in class and listen to what people have to say and then respond.

I personally feel more engaged during in class discussions, and enjoy the turn of events and elaboration on topics discussed.

Many students liked that they had the flexibility of when to go online, however they did not like that amount of time involved once online. For example, one student summed it up with, "It was very time consuming because I had to go online all week to make sure I did not miss any postings. "

More specifically, students reported that they liked the convenience, the breadth, depth and the record of responses. Regarding convenience ("being able to respond when it was convenient for me") students used such words as "freedom" and "independence." Regarding the breadth of comments, students commented, "that there were more responses to online reflections than in class" and "that we at least got to hear something form everyone, without the online format, a lot of people would have not shared as much about their experiences."

Regarding the record of the interaction students responded that, "If you forgot something that was said you could go back and refresh your memory before responding." Students also commented that they liked "the deeper discussions that took place" and "people responded more "in-depth."

The primary dislikes related to the time involved in reading and responding to reflections, the asynchronous nature of the format (e.g., the time lag between postings and responses), and some complained of the impersonal nature of the online format:

> It did take a long time sometimes to read the entries if there were a lot of new entries.

> I did not like the unstructured format, I felt like some people were posting very early in the week and some late in the week. I felt like I had to keep checking the site all of the time.

> It added several more hours of reading and writing a week and it often became difficult to keep up with new postings. I also found that sometimes there was a reach to comment on reflection as many people started running to sameness at practicum from week to week.

> I get more out of things if I hear discussions as opposed to reading them. Sometimes I wanted to ask a question and get a response/feedback. This often took a while to get. I like the back and forth conversation we get in the classroom that is not really possible online.

The feedback that I received as the instructor was to provide more guidance and structure. The requests ranged from, "Flag certain responses/experiences we should pay more attention to," to provide "more feedback regarding whether they were doing what I wanted them to be doing."

Another student wanted me to "Verify the accuracy of threads, and clarify the questions that I was asking."

In contrast, others commented that they thought my involvement and presence was adequate. One student even explained that, "I enjoyed the structured questions that were asked of everyone, they got me thinking a lot more."

Additional benefits

As students enter this profession they are building a community of knowledge about the school psychology profession. The blended format highlighted a collaborative nature. By submitting and responding to each other's reflections, students were bonding, building a community, collaborating on issues confronted and problem solving.

Many of the school psychology students (and faculty) are not technology fluent. However, the field is moving in the direction of using technology as a vehicle to provide services. Students who become more familiar and less intimidated with the new technology during their training years may broaden their experience in this realm when in the field.

> "Students who become more familiar and less intimidated with technology during their training years may broaden their experience in this realm when in the field."

Because the asynchronous discussion slows down discussion, I was better able to analyze what students know and how they interpret new information into their knowledge schemas. I was more aware of my role when formulating questions to hopefully provide students with opportunities to revise and improve the quality of their thinking and understanding related to topics that were activated for them by real life experience. The record of interactions also was a way to contain the community of school psychology.

Incorporating the online component into the practicum class encouraged me to reexamine my teaching philosophy, especially the design of learning environments and the role of collaborative learning. Comparing the online discussion to the in-class discussion provided me with an opportunity to view teaching from a different angle.

As I visited the myCourses site I thought of an example in Paulo Freire's *Pedagogy of the Oppressed,* regarding a teacher who entered the classroom at the beginning of a semester and sat in the back of the classroom in order to shake up the students' preconceptions regarding who is in charge of their learning. In a different way, the students, postings of their reflections allowed me to take a seat among my students and add to the discussion when I felt there was a need—to point out gaps, inconsistencies or provide a question that was within their zone of proximal development. No longer were the students predominantly looking to me when they were talking in class or expecting and waiting for me to respond. The talk time was more evenly distributed; power and responsibility was shared.

Modifications

Based on this experience, I believe the blended format enhances the learning experience for the practicum supervision. The question for me is no longer whether to use a blended format but how to modify it to the most effective configuration to supplement the classroom supervision.

Modifications to be made include:

- Meeting every other week online, rather than consecutive weeks
- Training on how to make reflections more user-friendly (i.e., having a subject title for each reflection, using HTML format, remembering to use spacing.)
- Explaining better about how to respond to reflections (i.e., not with one-word responses)
- Walking students through the myCourses site in class
- Responding to the threads rather than summarizing

Postscript

Over the last three years, the blended format has been fully integrated into all the field experience based classes that I teach. The blended format is not only well suited for these classes but has become an essential part of the class. The students appreciate that they do not need to come to campus to participate in the class. They also like the resource sharing. I like how students collaborate, use each other as resources and challenge each other on the topics. In addition to the resource sharing, there is a resource saving element to the experience in that the students save gas by not driving to campus, and save paper since they do not print out their reflection papers.

The blended format continues to provide me with a way to access the students' understanding of the issues, where they may have blocks and what they have learned. I also like the blended format for discovering what more of my students are thinking. I use this information to enhance the classroom experience and to encourage the low participators to participate.

Jennifer Lukomski is an associate professor in the school psychology department in the College of Liberal Arts.

Glossary

Adobe Presenter — An add-in installed as a menu item in Microsoft PowerPoint. The author can add their own voice narration with accompanying script. The viewer can start, stop, rewind or fast-forward the presentation at anytime. Not compatible with Mac software.

Asynchronous — a method of instructional delivery in which students can learn at any time from anywhere over the Internet.

Blog/weblog—a web-based online journal with short, dated posts listed in reverse chronological order.

Breeze and Connect web conferencing — A web-based communication tool that allows participants at different locations to meet in real-time and share audio and video discussion, PowerPoint presentations, whiteboards and text chat. Online Learning at RIT supports Adobe Connect (formerly Macromedia Breeze).

Chat session — A virtual, synchronous meeting using text to discuss topics with multiple people at once.

Class list — A directory of the names and e-mails of students in the class, allowing other students or the instructor quick access to contact them.

Clipboard survey tool — An online survey system, developed by Online Learning at RIT, that allows instructors to set up, deliver and evaluate surveys with a user-friendly, web-based tool.

Course management system (CMS) — A tool that allows the development, support and delivery of online and blended learning. RIT uses myCourses as it's course management system.

Desire2Learn — The vendor that provides the "template" for myCourses, RIT's courseware management system. A competitor to the Blackboard CMS.

Discussion forum — An area of myCourses in which students can engage in asynchronous discussion on various topics, usually set up by the instructor.

Dropbox — A submission box into which students electronically submit assignments for evaluation.

First Class — The first courseware management system used at Rochester Institute of Technology. A forerunner to myCourses, it was used exclusively for online courses from 1997 to 2007.

Gradebook — An online grading tool in myCourses that allows both instructor and student to see overall grades and individual assignments.

Locker — An area in myCourses where students can upload and store files.

myCourses — Web-based software used at RIT that is primarily used to facilitate instruction of blended and online courses. It has many features, including the classlist, news, gradebook, locker, chat, dropbox, etc.

News feature —A section on the home page of every myCourses course shell in which instructors can post various items. It's often used to keep students on track with each week's goals and expected deliverables.

Online learning — A learning environment that uses the Internet as the delivery vehicle, synonymous with e-learning.

Online Learning department — The department at Rochester Institute of Technology responsible for the delivery and support of online, blended and technology-enhanced courses. For more, see online.rit.edu.

Pachyderm — An online multimedia production tool, designed for users with little multimedia experience.

Pager — A user-friendly tool in myCourses that informs students and instructors who's online at any time and enables them to contact others in real-time, similar to instant messaging.

Second Life — An online virtual world. Users are represented by human-like avatars, which the user can customize to their liking. The Second Life world consists of islands paid for and constructed by commercial, non-profit and educational entities.

Synchronous — Communication in which interaction between parties takes place simultaneously in real-time. Also used in reference to real-time web conferencing or teleconferencing.

Teleconferencing — Telephone networking that allows groups of learners at several locations to communicate with the instructor and each other through a synchronous exchange of audio, video or text (or a combination).

Webcam — A small video camera used to share images and video through Internet messaging or a computer video conferencing application.

Author Index

B
Barnes, Susan — 76
Bierre, Kevin — 86
Brenyo, James — 15
Bruening, Eric — 49

C
Castelli, Fabio Escobar — 140
Chung, Bob — 166
Coffey, Birgit — 19
Conley, Pamela — 124
Cos, Grant — 83
Cox, Nicole — 168
Craig. Paul — 178
Crawford, Kijana — 201

D
DeCotis, Paul — 191
Doane, Paula — 115
Doolittle, Richard — 174

E
Elahi, Babak — 146

F
Farrar, John — 61
Feeney Bushnell, Eileen — 159
Fredrick, Kristine — 130

G
Gilbert, Tim — 182
Graney, Suzanne — 188

H
Hauser, Peter — 204
Henneky, Joseph — 99
Hermsen, Lisa — 79

J
Jacobs, Stephen — 95

K
Keiner, Christine — 143
Kepler, Jill — 154
Kim, Spencer Seung — 185
Kleper, Michael — 164

L
Lawley, Elizabeth — 109
Ludi, Stephanie — 102
Lukomski, Jennifer — 214
Lutz, Michael — 91

M
Mallory, James — 121
Manzi, Peter — 210
Mason, Sharon — 88
Mittler, Todd — 30
Monikowski, Christine — 112
Mortimer, Ian — 36

N
N'Da, Koffi — 10
Neely, Pam — 23

P
Porter, Judy — 196
Pritchard, David — 28
Pugliese, Rudy — 73

R
Reichlmayer, Tom — 106
Retallack, John — 64

S
Samar, Vincent	117
Santana, Richard	149
Stone, Thomas	134
Striebich, John	45

T
Traub, Thomas	57

W
Ward, John	53
Woelk, Ben	70
Wollan, Patricia	41